1985

BOOKS BY LEONARD GROSS

GOD AND FREUD

THE LAST, BEST HOPE

1985

1985

An Argument for Man

BY LEONARD GROSS

W · W · NORTON & COMPANY · INC ·
NEW YORK

"They'll reach the peak, they'll eat, they'll drink with heavy minds, their dull hearts will be twined with fat, their seed will choke, and then, my God, another Archer will spring on earth!

"Our stock is strong! Don't be distressed, God, we shall free you! 'How long will this game last?' you ask. To the world's end!"

— *The Odyssey: A Modern Sequel* by Nikos Kazantzakis

CONTENTS

Is the world really worse off than ever—or is our sense of its problems simply more acute and courageous?

Before we succumb to the first possibility, we should at least examine the second.

Dear Linden, Dear Jeff

I dedicated my first book to your mother, and my second to mine. The more I learned about this one, the more inadequate it seemed just to mention your names on a frontispiece, along with some words of love. I realized that I was writing this book not simply for, but because of you.

I address you in 1970, at the age of forty-two. While that figure looks pretty good on actuarial tables and I have never felt better, I must inform you that among the age group you will shortly join, I am twelve years dead. So I hasten to offer you this accounting while you still afford me the awe and respect due the family champion in the twenty-yard dash.

Please, first, accept a father's gratitude for the precocious grace with which you absorbed the several disruptions I forced upon your lives. There's a widespread notion that children adjust to foreign countries as easily as babies learn to swim. I held that stupid notion the first time out. I imagined that, through some magical osmosis, you would be speaking Portuguese within weeks after we'd reached Brazil. Linden, I recall how confidently we enrolled you in first grade at a Brazilian school and how beautifully you did at first. Ninety-eight, 100, 94, said the papers you brought home. Then, one by one, your foreign classmates transferred to other schools, until you were a lone American in a class of Brazilian kids. At that point, the teacher shifted into high gear, and soon the papers you brought home were marked 36, 14, 22, 9, and your mother and I realized that you just couldn't understand. Nor was the school equipped to help you.

Basically, your options will be three. You can work within the System, and try to make it better. Or you can try to tear the System down and put something else in its place. Or, despairing of your chances of changing anything, you can tune out the world—retreating to what Sir Isaiah Berlin calls the "inner citadel" of the self through ascetic insights or drugs.

You'll forgive me, I hope, if I admit that, for your mother and me, great stakes ride on your choice. You are our extension in time. What you do with your lives validates —or invalidates—our own in a way that nothing else can.

Linden, when you were very young, you asked me, "What do we believe?" I laughed and hugged you and told you that while I could tell you what I believed, I wanted you to work out your beliefs for yourself. "But I want to believe what you believe," you protested, and I laughed and hugged you again.

I haven't changed my attitude, but I *have* developed some hopes. And because the world has changed so much since then, I've also developed some fears. What I fear most is that on your return to the U.S., you could be caught up in that monstrous indulgence that grips our land, wherein your age group tells mine we have nothing to discuss. That kind of thought cleaves children from parents. Love flows from respect; I choose not to forfeit yours.

One of the great troubles with our concepts today is that in the clash between those who are coming of age and those who run the world an entire generation has been all but overlooked. As a consequence we have misgauged the velocity of change.

Once this missing generation has been fitted into reality, then we see that we may not be in the midst of a revolution at all, but in a period of vigorous, consistent, and vital—if occasionally dangerous, senseless, and heartbreaking—transition. Historians in some calmer epoch may very well conclude that the challenge today's young generation has leveled at society actually originated in mine.

We may be the most underrated generation of recent times. We have been overlooked by the young visionaries who want a new society and do not realize that if they are to have it, it is we who must help them make it. They talk as though there is nothing between them and their Establishment targets, the old fossils in their fifties, sixties, and seventies who are running the universities and the government. But there is most definitely something—a generation uniquely fitted by temperament and circumstance to act as an effective bridge between warring social factions.

We have been underrated for more than twenty years, ever since someone characterized us as "the Silent Generation," and mentally cast us aside. It may have been an accurate label then; it could hardly apply today. We have reversed the traditional process whereby today's progressive becomes tomorrow's conservative. Instead of fossilizing, our generation has radicalized.

If we began in silence, it was with good reason. We had come of age in a state of shock. No sooner had we geared down emotionally from our commitment to the war against fascism, than we were asked to gear up again for a war against communism. Questions that can be asked today were not asked then. In the few years it took us to finish college, the Soviet Union manipulated itself into control of Eastern Europe, the Communists took China, and Communist North Korea invaded South Korea. There was no subterfuge then; nothing was devious; everything seemed simple and open. Once again, we warred against aggression.

Later, the doubts began. Today, there is enough balance

in our society for scholars to ask whether some of the blame for the Cold War should not be lodged with us. But then, passion had the floor and Joseph R. McCarthy was giving his name to some years of U.S. history. No one who is in his early twenties now can imagine what it was like to be in his early twenties then. Many of us protested the pervasive hysteria he represented; but we were awed and stricken and, I suppose, finally crushed by the sight of the Senate and the Army and even the President of the United States being manhandled by a demagogue. It was sickening. Lives were ruined, careers shattered. Neighbor turned on neighbor. It produced a species of reasoning that would have been comic had it not been tragic. I recall the moments after the Notre Dame-North Carolina game at Yankee Stadium in 1949. The Tarheels, undefeated underdogs, had held the Irish to a first-half tie; in the second half they'd been crushed. As the crowd spilled onto the field, a red-faced rooter with a Southern accent shook his fist at the departing Notre Dame players and shouted, *"God-damned Communists!"* He could not have been more serious.

So my generation worked hard to make up for the lost years; it learned its lessons, built its homes, bore its children, and kept its mouth closed.

The public mistook silence for emptiness. In creative terms, we were not the Silent Generation at all. The Private Generation would be a much more accurate phrase. As the public shouting grew more inane and vulgar, the private dialogue rose in quality and extended in range. Surely, as William Styron has said, we were the most mistrustful of power and the least nationalistic of any generation that America had yet produced. The mood was contagious; we questioned everything—archaic politics, antique economics, rigid education, destructive sexual and social relations. Our doubts expressed themselves best in a literature that utilized, as never before, the symptoms of alienation and discontent. If we did not write all of this literature, it was we through whom it all passed. One way or another, we discovered that we had become something we did not wish to be. And we sought to do something about it. Our generation did not simply adapt to change; it embraced and even provoked it.

Our method was not confrontation. It was an invention that history may list as genius.

We listened.

If silence was our distinguishing characteristic it was also, by God, our virtue. The requisite to listening is silence; until you can listen, you can't understand. Precisely because we were silent, we could appreciate the protests and pleas, the reason and sense that others could or would not understand before. That understanding uncovered the intellectual bedrock on which change is building today.

But we did something beyond that—and if there is a lost beat to the pace of change, it is here.

As new visions matured in us, we raised a new generation in those images. We gave you a chance we never really had, a chance to be yourselves. Before you could act, you required the visions; it was these you received from us. You then took our visions—or fantasies, if you please—and sought to make them real.

The biological connection between us is self-evident. What has been poorly perceived is this thought, this attitude, this understanding that links us. Change did not miraculously spring from earth. My generation plowed the ground for that growth.

I have been a chronicler of that process, and I confess it

has produced a bias. I am against retreats to inner citadels, against destruction, and for mammoth quantities of change. I hope you work through the System, and I hope you change it a lot.

Your peers will tell you that this makes me a hypocrite, like eveyone else over thirty; that the System is so rotten, change through its processes is impossible; that the only way to save the world is to tumble the structure and start anew. They will offer you heroes like Che and Mao and Marcuse, whom most of them will not have read. I often wonder whether the cry of some of our protesters for a system so vulnerable to tyranny is not the unconscious yearning for the authority they missed at home. A child with unlimited freedom gets frightened; he suspects he isn't loved.

Yet a child with more freedom than any of us has ever possessed before—freedom from want, freedom to think, study, care—is free to do what has never been possible before, either because men never dared do it before, or else never dreamed that they could. Somewhere between the extremes of anarchy and authority lies a new means of marrying personal freedom to public good.

I can't certify your future. I don't know for sure that you'll have one. Do you know what it means for a father to say that? My rage and my shame are reserved for the knowledge that the conditions you will inherit from me do not guarantee you a peaceful destiny.

You belong to a generation that does not believe in its future. That is the simplest, soundest explanation for the anarchic wave awash in the world. You will be swept up by that wave, urged to let go, out, turn away. You will find a generation disgusted with what it perceives, rightly or wrongly, as America—a military fortress, permanently armed, whose business is to kill. When you create that kind of enterprise you can believe it will find uses for itself. And your outraged group says to hell with that enterprise.

And I say hallelujah.

But I say, as well, recognize what it is that you are seeing:

That this military fortress is not what we were, and not what we will be if those of us against it persist, but some temporary aberrant, some jagged crevice along man's historic path.

That this anarchic, nihilist doomsday reaction to our militarization is not what we were and not what we will be, but some natural, normal, and necessary reaction in self-defense.

That to judge what men are like today, you must note not simply the graves they have dug for themselves, but their determined effort to climb out.

What I *can* do, and propose to do now, is to tell you what I've learned about reality, and what I have learned about change. Change—reactionary, orderly, revolutionary—has been my story. My experiences have given me a feeling about reality that, today, is not widely shared.

There is no argument whatever about what we all want: peace, justice, an end to suffering in all forms. What seems to set me apart from many of my colleagues—and possibly qualifies me as a museum piece—is my belief that you, and even I, may see these dreams come true.

All of the necessary mechanisms for these changes are already known to man. What is crucial to progress is belief that it can occur, and what is crucial to *that* belief is man's belief in himself.

I'm sure you remember Sydney Gruson, thanks to whose presence in Paris I did not have to buy a golf ball for the better part of two years. One day while he was still editor and publisher of the international edition of *The New York Times*, he and I had lunch together, along with Henry Tanner, then the *Times* Paris bureau chief. We argued about the nature of man. Sydney insisted that man was inherently evil. I insisted that, while the capacity for evil existed in man, man was inherently good. Henry sided with Sydney. That was the moment I realized how vastly different working patterns within the same profession could fashion diametrical views of man. They deal, primarily, with crises, and with men who create or solve them. Because news is largely a distortion of what is normal, they tend to see men and events and, ultimately, history itself, as a continuous process of agitation. I have dealt with crises, too, but my eye has been fixed primarily on the gathering fabric of society, not the thrusts of the weaving needle.

I contend—and will try to prove—that the thrusting needle and the gathering fabric represent contradictory, yet compatible, elements of modern society.

The thrusting needle symbolizes our terrifying, apocalyptic age.

The gathering fabric symbolizes man's increasing power to direct the needle—not simply with a scientific and technological mastery that sets the last twenty years apart from the last twenty thousand, but in the moral and ethical ways that could enable man, at last, to control his political, social, and economic environment.

We live in a period when every old form of authority (including the authority of fathers) is undergoing challenge from within its ranks. These simultaneous, strident, abundant challenges have created an atmosphere of apparent moral breakdown. I will try to show that the headlines of chaos may actually be the warp and woof of an emerging and desirable consensus; that the sounds of clamor are actually the beginnings of dialogue between men who twenty years ago either could not or would not speak to one another, and could not give common meanings to the same words if they did; men of varying persuasions, races, and nationalities; men who forsake the rhetoric of ideology for the nomenclature of solutions; men who start from opposite poles, but converge on a common center.

I will try to show, finally, that what gives symmetry and coherence to this dialogue is a shared conception of what it means to be a man—that the individual, fully realized, is becoming the common denominator of genuine democratic and revolutionary movements to an extent that was unimaginable only a few years ago. The determination of the individual to gain, or regain, his individuality, to wrest his uniqueness from governments and societies, systems and institutions, is the prime cause of the clamor that is the disturbing, but pivotal stage of man's evolution to freedom.

The most foolish lie I could tell you is that this evolution is assured. It is as fragile and vulnerable and helpless as you were as babies, and like you would have, it will die without love and care. It has started late in a race against other forces that are dehumanizing, conservative, and mechanistic. Can it win? I could be so very wrong, but I really think it can. I hesitate to transfer the burden, but to a very small extent, the outcome depends on you. And what you do about it, as I've suggested, will depend on whether you believe that man is decent, that progress is possible, and that the world is improving, not ending.

Dad

Paris,
June 15, 1970

CHAPTER ONE

TRUTH IS ROUND

Is the world really worse off than ever, or is our sense of its problems simply more acute and courageous?

Before we succumb to the first possibility, we should at least examine the second.

I have no illusions about the state of the world. If I had ever had them, twenty years of the kind of travel and experience I have had in forty different countries would have dispelled them. I've been with people whose daily meal comes from the garbage dumps of Santiago, and whose homes are built atop their source of food. I've been to an Iranian village 80 percent of whose inhabitants are blinded by trachoma. I've stood on the Nile watching women draw drinking water a few yards from a wading, urinating cow. I've watched men dig for crabs at low tide in polluted Brazilian rivers. We call it the crab cycle: man eats crab, crab eats man. Later, at home, the man stands, sapped by amoebas, beside his child of two. The child's belly is bloated. A bloated belly means death. Still later, when he bears the tiny wooden coffin to its grave, the man will cry. But he will not suffer long. By thirty, he, too, will be dead.

So I have seen what underdevelopment means in terms of human suffering in a way that most people haven't, and in attempting to learn how suffering can be alleviated, I have learned how deeply the problem is interwoven with insensitivity and greed.

Sometimes, the speed of our times drives these exposures into my heart with a force that makes it falter. I left that Iranian village early one afternoon in 1960 and drove in a jeep to an airport on the Persian Gulf. There I met an Iranian prince. We flew together to Teheran. After we changed, he took me to a dark nightclub and introduced me to his cousins. Since Iranian law once permitted a man four wives, everyone in the upper class is everyone else's cousin. Six of his were there, sitting with pretty girls, French dancers in the city to do a show. Later the girls would entertain their escorts; my benefactor told me he had been with every one of them, and he pointed out which girl had been the best. On the table were bottles of Scotch—Black Label. Eight hours after I had left the village of blind people, my first course was set before me. It was a bowl of caviar.

I remember an evening at an Argentine *estancia*—one of those lush ranches in the *pampa* where cattle graze in grass that grows, unfertilized, to their knees. The *estancia* was owned by a beautiful woman whose husband had been killed in an airplane crash several years before. The husband had been a crack polo player; when Prince Philip would come to Argentina, he would play polo at this ranch, and live in a splendid guest house, where I was now put up. The woman had six superb-looking daughters, one of whom had just married; the night of my visit, she was there with her new husband, a tall and amiable fellow who owned a neighboring *estancia*. We spoke of Fidel Castro and unrest in Latin America, and he said quite openly and honestly, "We want to keep things as they are."

I have seen how "things" are kept "as they are"—the selfish decisions and lack of vision on the part of controlling powers, and the absence of any moral or social force to make them change their ways. I know how these men, as their fathers and fathers before them, use government as a game, how in states of chronic dollar imbalances, officials will even permit the sale of government treasury dollars to friends so they may import luxuries, travel abroad, or simply profit from black-market exchange. Worse, because these men are without a social conscience, they do not comprehend their wrong.

Against such human inertia, even a highly motivated reform government may often be ineffective, because it can easily be paralyzed by jealous politicians on both its left and right. I have witnessed the Christian Democratic government of Chile's Eduardo Frei whipsawed by Communists and reactionaries whose only basis for unity was the desire to see him fail.

I know that our own government, in the name of anti-Communism, has acted wittingly and unwittingly to perpetuate reactionaries, that every practice ascribed to Russia's KGB is known to our own CIA as well. Once there was a leftist prisoner in a certain country who was very religious and asked frequently to see priests. One day a CIA employee dressed as a priest went to his cell and, as the U.S. foreign service officer who told me the story put it, "administered last rites." I believe there is some merit to the charge that we have become an instinctive counterrevolutionary force, to the point where we crush even those legitimate democratic uprisings against dictatorship that are controlled by staunch non-Communist progressives, simply because of our obsessive fears that the few Communists among them might seize power. Our intrusion in the Dominican Republic is a perfect case in point.

One day in 1968, Senator William Fulbright told the

Congress that since World War II, and in the name of anti-
Communism, our government had spent $904 billion as of
late 1967 on military power. At the same time we had spent
only $96 billion from the regular national budget on educa-
tion, health, welfare, housing and community development.
By our military expenditures we bought the containment of
Russian ambitions, but whatever was spent in excess of that
need cost us, in good part, the fearful domestic problems before which we tremble today—as well as a measure of the
world's contempt.

While I have lived abroad for seven of the last nine
years, I have lived most of my life in the U.S. and have returned to it often enough in recent years to know well the nature of despair in my own country. I know that I have been the
envy of many friends, who in the darkest moments of 1968
talked seriously to me of emigration, change of citizenship—
and shame. I know the hate that rages in some white hearts and
the rage it arouses in black. Our whites, who began to emigrate to the suburbs after World War II, are now fleeing the
cities in torrents; if this trend continues, we may very well
see realized the joint prophecy of Urban America and the
Urban Coalition, that we will be "two societies, black and
white, increasingly separate and scarcely less unequal." The
United States today ranks first among the seventeen Western
democracies in total magnitude of civil strife, according to
our National Commission on the Causes and Prevention of
Violence. Powerful social pressures of big-city living are transforming Americans into potential assassins, according to a
Stanford University research psychologist. The conclusions
may or may not be too broad for the research, but the study
brought to mind a tour of the United States I made in 1964,
after thirty-eight neighbors in Queens failed to heed the cries
for help of a dying girl named Kitty Genovese. I wrote

an article called "Who Cares?"; I found that many Americans
did not.

I have reported frequently on our more subtle brands of
cruelty to one another—and because of a prolonged fascina-
tion with the subjects of psychiatry and psychology, I have
learned a little about man's cruelty to himself.

So I will stipulate here and now that the available evidence is against me, that the world, as we know it, is foul.

By what reckoning, then, do I retain my faith in man?

Man decent? Progress possible? The world improving?
Ideas like these belong to dreamy bygone days; in our modern age of looming cataclysm they are logically suspect and
fashionably *gauche*. The great majority of our columnists expose our foibles; the few graced with humor mock them.

There was a period toward the end of the nineteenth
century when society basked in a view widely shared among
communicators that man could equal his aims. Today the
opposite is true.

Pessimism is "in," despair further "in." Our arts, as well
as our journals, document the political, social, moral, and
aesthetic demise of man. Theatrical obscurities, cinematic
fragments, naïve, overt plastic art forms are deliberately illogical statements structured to mirror man's bewilderment
with contemporary life.

Now, no one does a great deal of anything unless it
provides some pleasure. While our creators would vehemently
deny it, their "dark perceptions" are arguably the natural
evolution, in sophisticated guise, of fundamentalist convic-
tions about man. When the preacher told man he was evil,
man set his mouth grimly or rolled in the aisle. But in his
heart he loved it. He knew for sure where he stood; if he
was a predetermined sinner, then he could rut with pleasure.

In a perverse and unconscious way, we love the wickedness theorem, too. We may have outgrown fundamentalist views of personal behavior, but we continue to think of man as a political sinner. It is neat and logical and fitting. If we are all, by nature, bastards, then that explains the world.

A remorseless trend sustains the dark view. When in a single year Martin Luther King and Robert Kennedy were assassinated, our troops burned civilians in Vietnam, the Russians crushed freedom in Czechoslovakia, Biafran children starved to death, and Chicago police brutalized youngsters, what good could be said of man—or his world or its future?

So despairing has man become of his nature and his fate that despair, itself, has become an active factor—a phenomenon that feeds on itself. Mounting despair makes men more nervous; more nervous men make more despair.

A society's belief in itself is, logically, the sum of personal beliefs held by its members. A proper dollop of narcissism, the psychiatrists tell us, is an essential element in the makeup of any healthy human being. Before he is capable of loving or believing in others, he must first be able to love and believe in himself. In a society where the worth of man is so persistently questioned, the development of a healthy degree of narcissistic acceptance becomes difficult, if not impossible. Not only are we influenced by the prevalent social perception; like the rutting sinners of fundamentalist days, we use the conviction of wickedness as an excuse to indulge our weakness.

Ever since Plato, man has tried to create a social order in which the chores that sustain him would be minimized and he would be free—to enjoy life, to reflect on the world, improve himself, and serve. We've come closer than anyone, and the closer our people get the more miserable they become. We have arrived at the Affluence of Dismay.

Any man who knows the stock market will tell you that the ideal time to buy is the day when most people sell. Perhaps the time has come to invest some belief in man.

Many years ago John Steinbeck paid a visit to Prague. He meandered about that exquisite and tragic medieval city with actors, gypsies, vagabonds, and others for whom he possessed such an affinity. During the same period, Steinbeck recounts in *Travels with Charley,* Joseph Alsop, "the justly famous critic of places and events," was also in Prague. He spent his time talking to diplomats, government officials, and other "informed people," and read innumerable reports. "Joe and I flew home to America in the same plane," Steinbeck recalls, "and on the way he told me about Prague, and his Prague had no relation to the city I had seen and heard. It just wasn't the same place, and yet each of us was honest, neither one a liar, both pretty good observers by any standard, and we brought home two cities, two truths."

What each may actually have brought home was a portion of a larger truth. Only when the two stories were fitted together could truth itself be approached.

A prime source for a journalist abroad is a diplomat at a friendly Embassy. In the case of U.S. journalists, that often means U.S. diplomats. Where the diplomat has the freedom to operate, he can be a great help. Where he is restricted, as in Communist countries, he is not much help at all. In the extreme case, he may be receiving impressions from journalists who are getting theirs from him. The result in that instance is what might be called "whifflebird journalism"—named after the bird that flies in ever tighter circles until it disappears up its own behind.

It is a simple matter for a journalist to "prove" almost anything he believes. A close examination of the structure of a "documented" piece of journalism will reveal an all but inevitable sequence of statement, example, statement, example. Since there is invariably one example or quotation to "prove" almost any thesis imaginable, almost any thesis can appear to be sustained.

Since news, by and large, chronicles events that distort the status quo, the morning newspaper or the evening television newscast present the collective distortion of what is normal at that given moment in the world. The exacerbating presence of the media, moreover, tends to augment the sense of distortion itself. I remember a Sunday morning brunch on the Ile St. Louis terrace of Edgar May, watching the barges slip along the Seine, when our friend James Jones, the novelist, told the following story:

One evening when he was in New York, an apartment building caught fire; a small crowd of whites and blacks gathered to watch in silence. Then up rolled a television crew. Blacks crowded in front of the camera, shouting, "Up yours, Whitey," and "We're gonna give it to you, Honky." After thirty minutes of such exposures, the television crew returned to mid-Manhattan. Once more, the crowd of whites and blacks quietly watched the fire.

Ed May, who won a Pulitzer Prize in 1961 for his stories on poverty before joining Sargent Shriver in government, told a story about a neighboring city. He could not find enough witnesses to make a case that would stick, he said, but he, personally, was convinced that an American tragedy had occurred in the following manner. In the midst of a summer riot, a news photographer for a major publication saw a black youth emerging from a looted store with a case of beer. He hailed the boy and asked him to go back inside and reenact the looting. God knows what possessed the boy, but he did it. As he was emerging, a police car rounded the corner. The boy ran. A policeman fired. The boy fell dead.

The prevailing description of the human condition is further affected by an unconscious process of selection on the part of the reporter, who, despite the best intentions, gravitates toward the anecdotes or quotations that confirm his—and, often his colleagues'—initial ideas.

I remember one particularly heartbreaking illustration, a day in 1963 in São Paulo, Brazil, where reporters had gathered to cover the second annual review meeting of the Alliance for Progress.

I arrived just after noon on the first day, but others had arrived earlier, and the "line" was out: the Alliance for Progress was dead. It seemed all the more heartbreaking because many of the reporters present had never visited an Alliance project. I asked one of them, a syndicated writer, if he too believed that the Alliance was dead. "Let's put it this way," he said. "The Alliance was stillborn." A while later a Brazilian journalist, a popular young fellow often consulted by other journalists for his views, approached. "You know the story of this conference?" he said. "The Alliance for Progress is dead, but everyone is afraid to write the obituary." Five minutes later a third journalist, who habitually depended upon the views of the second, whispered in my ear: "I am writing the obituary of the Alliance for Progress."

Seven years have passed since that incident. The Alliance for Progress has survived nine years of its projected ten-year life-span. It has failed to transform the countries of Latin America into models of democracy, as its American creators naïvely assumed it would; one cannot, after all, invite the beneficiaries of the status quo to officiate at its demolition. But the Alliance has brought water to 5,600 communities and to 1,401,000 acres that did not previously have it; reclaimed through clearance 1,767,000 acres; provided technical assistance in tax administration that has vastly increased tax collections; helped foster 11,000 new cooperatives; benefited one million families through new land tenure policies (in Colombia alone, in 1969, 80,000 families were purchasing their own farms under a new government program, and the gross annual income of the average small farmer had more than doubled in two years); all but doubled the miles of roads in Latin America; stimulated a 117 percent increase in the number of primary-school graduates and a 184 percent increase in the number of secondary-chool graduates; created 37,063 classrooms and invested $176,000,000 in seed capital for housing. The human feedback from this effort can never be calculated. Nor can the negative impact of the death sentences passed by journalists on a program in the second year of a ten-year life.

Once in awhile, a story results from pressure applied by an editor who is understandably anxious to prove the validity of his decision to undertake the story—particularly if the idea for the story was his. Perhaps the worst abuse of this technique I have ever seen was a story written during the "sophisticated muckraking" days of the *Saturday Evening Post* about the Communist threat in Latin America. Certainly, Communists were present, in every style known—Maoists, Castroites, Moscow-liners. Some believed in violent overthrow, others in popular fronts, still others in ultimate victory through the elective process. To say that these elements represented one of several permanent political forces that would ultimately compel change—as has recently happened in Chile—was a legitimate, sustainable thesis; to say that these elements were about to imprison Latin America in their totalitarian clasp was not. Yet by knitting together every shred, element, quotation, and incident on which it could gain its hand, the *Post* seemed to sustain its thesis that Latin America was imperiled by Communist seizures.

Anyone with knowledge of the area knew that this simply wasn't so, that, at that moment, and for the foreseeable future, not a single country—not even Bolivia, where Che Guevara would later try—was vulnerable to a Communist *coup*. Yet, using the sequence of statement, example, statement, example, statements unevaluated, examples not placed in context, the *Post* "proved" Latin America's vulnerability.

A year later, I met one of the writers at a party. To my surprise—and dismay—he volunteered an apology for the work. "We kept calling New York and telling them it wasn't there, but they insisted on the story."

One of the principal figures on whom the *Post* had based its case had been a self-styled Marxist named Francisco Julião, who had been forming peasants' leagues in Brazil's Northeast. A *Look* photographer, Douglas Jones, and I had spent a week with Julião in February of 1961, traveling the barren country in a jeep; we departed with what we considered a valid profile of a Latin American revolutionary type. Several weeks later, our story was laid out in New York, and ready for inclusion in a package about South America.

One day at this time, my editor, Dan Mich, and I were invited to lunch by two executives of *Look,* to meet the vice-president of a large American corporation with extensive commitments in Brazil. The man was concerned about the possibility of a Castro-style takeover in the country, and the precise focus of his concern was Julião, about whom he'd been reading in *The New York Times.* He wanted my assessment.

I said that in my opinion, the two situations were not comparable. Julião was phlegmatic, scholarly, physically depleted, no match for the virile activist Castro. Brazil's leftist government at that time was led by a mercurial reformist from São Paulo, Jânio Quadros, who had no intention of being overridden by a small-time *Nordestino*. The Brazilian Establishment, while negligent and incompetent and genially corrupt, was not (then) the vicious sadistic killer government of Batista. The terrain was so vast as to defeat any guerrilla force. The peasants were as depleted as their leader. No, I said, Julião would be no Brazilian Castro.

The executive seemed reassured. So gracious were his compliments that by the time Dan Mich and I left the dining room together, I was all but calculating my raise. We had not walked twenty feet when Dan said to me, "I'm sending you back to Brazil."

I was stunned. "Why?" I said.

"On the basis of what you said, I can't print that story."

"But it's a classic study of a Latin American revolutionary."

"That's true. But because it's the only story we're running on Brazil in the issue, the reader will remember *that* as Brazil. And you've just told me that's not Brazil, it's just a part."

The next week I returned to Brazil; several weeks later, we printed a two-spread, four-page story. The second spread offered a contrast; *The South: Booming. The North: Dying.* Our pictorial symbol for the South was a mulatto foundry worker rolling up a sleeve. Our symbol for the North was the frail revolutionary, Julião. I stated that if he tried revolution he would fail. Two years later, in the military coup of 1964, Julião was captured and jailed.

I had learned my lesson—the best of many Dan Mich taught me. It was this:

Truth is rarely a fixed point. The morning's headline is a morsel of truth, but until it becomes a part of the historical framework, it is conceivably misleading and unquestionably incomplete.

Truth consists of many parts, some of which may appear to be in contradiction.

If truth can be conceived of as possessing geometric property, then truth is not a point, or even a line. Truth is round.

Let's look now at truth in the round. Let's examine the clamor and see what has caused it—and consider whether our vision of perdition may not in fact be a signal of redemption.

Judge reality by your morning newspaper or evening newscast and despair becomes your metaphor. But judge it against reality as it existed twenty, thirty, fifty years ago and hope begins to stir. Then you see that the world may not be ending after all; it may be—it just *may be*—moving irresistibly toward those qualities of life to which men of goodwill aspire.

Think of truth as a round and moving mass, whose contours distort from the force of motion, whose contents change with the force of time, casting off the vestigial past (often with the flame and violence with which a star throws off a meteor), magnetizing the pertinent future.

It is this truth of seeming contradictions, encompassing violence, synthesis, and change, that locates us in the geography of time. Only by knowing where we've been can we determine where we are.

Civilizations have died throughout history, and it is no great trick for those who remain fundamentalists in the bowels of their minds to make the case for the impending death of ours. But if morals are to be drawn let us draw them not from the dot of an incident or even the line of a running story, but from the roundness in which they are born.

These are *different* times. The *International Herald Tribune* has neatly summed up why:

> There is a quality in the world's atmosphere today to chal-lenge any authority, whether of church, state or political party, a ferment which knows no geographical boundaries, a spirit which is far more comprehensive, and far-reaching than that of 1789, or 1848 or even of 1917.
>
> And the corollary of this is that authority will resist the challenge. . . . This can hardly come as a surprise; established orders would not be long established if they did not fight back. What makes the present situation exceptional is not the fact of the reply, but the nature of the challenge . . .

We are asking all the right questions at last. *That* is the nature of the challenge, and *that* is a basis for hope. Some questions arise from necessity, others from an ultimate form of disgust. Whatever their origin, their existence and inten-sity measure the extent to which man is approaching freedom. These questions are so threatening and persistent that they compel and provoke replies. That is a kind of dialogue such as has never occurred before. What is implicit in all of these dialogues is something that is vastly more important than any of their parts. The common subject of revolutionary dialogue is a new image of man. The common effort is an attempt to humanize the dehumanizing forces of life.

History is, in large part, the story of man's willingness— even desire—to come to terms with the reality he inherits. Authority has always before been a psychological security. It defined boundaries within which man could exist. The psychological compulsion for this desire is described by Erich Fromm in his recent book, *The Revolution of Hope:*

. . . man finds his emotional ties to a superior authority, which he blindly obeys. . . . Inasmuch as man has to work within a given society, his need for survival tends to make him accept the social conceptualizations and hence to repress that which he would be aware of had his consciousness been imprinted with different schemata.

What makes these times so different is that man appears to be breaking out of this very self-imposed prison. The challenge to authority is a signal that man is at last seeking, not escaping from freedom.

I am writing now very early on a beautiful fall morning in Paris. The house is quiet. Last night, I talked to a colleague who has just moved to Paris. He is a brilliant reporter. He has witnessed bitter reality. He, too, is writing a book. His will be pessimistic. He asked about mine. I told him I was hopeful. "Where?" he demanded. "What countries?"

It is not countries. It is ideas. It is man and ideas transcending countries. Ultimately, of course, it concerns countries, and institutions and generations and race. But at its very base, it concerns how men felt about themselves until only very recently—and how they feel today.

CHAPTER TWO

THE POLITICS OF SEX

When I was twelve my father took me for a long walk one Sunday late in the fall, and put the matter bluntly: "How much do you know?" I told him what little I did know; he thought it was a lot. He told me then when that time came that I would want a girl, I should come to him for "protection." And then he explained that, whereas, in sexual intercourse, semen issued naturally because its conduit was properly heated by the female enclosure, masturbation did not produce such heat and therefore weakened a man.

I worshiped my father, and he was no fool. But I do his memory no dishonor when I suggest that we are light years removed today from the well-meaning nonsense on which he and his generation were raised.

During the 1950s, someone invented something called Togetherness. He surely never dreamed that by the end of the 60s, Togetherness would be parents and children sitting shoulder to shoulder watching naked people shouting expletives at a performance of *Hair*. Thirty years after my father and I took our private walk, our family—and a capacity London audience—heard the melodic advice that "Masturbation . . . can be fun."

I loved that show—its beat, its humor, its honesty, its celebration of life and love and its unremitting attack on inanity and hypocrisy. But I would be less than honest if I did not admit that each time some actor uttered words whose meanings I had learned from dictionaries, or grabbed another's private parts, or one of those parts came in view, my eyes moved from the stage to each of my children's faces.

I operate on the conviction that nothing my children might see or hear or read could hurt them as much as would my refusal to let them see or hear or read it. That's a satisfying sentence to write, but I know that there are times when, to keep faith with my conviction, I must grit my teeth. Everything goes today, and with it, the balanced view. So there has been a time when, after a series of particularly horrendous movies about man's seamy sexual side, I've had to announce that, surprising as it may seem, there *are* occasions when love is something that occurs between two people of opposite sex who get married and, in the ultimate expression of this love, conceive and nurture children.

But that night in London, I knew that whatever plip of conflict my children's sex education might arouse in my own conditioned past, the effort was more than worth it. As we walked out of that theater and into Soho, I felt I was passing from the promise of the future into the rot of the past. Soho is one of Western civilization's larger garbage dumps, littered with furtive, guilt-ridden men succumbing to what they had been taught all their lives were base and vile instincts. There they stood now, fighting their private wars, peering into stores at dirty books, or inspecting "French models" perched at their windows, waiting for them to call the telephone numbers prominently displayed in the phone booths below; or grouped uncertainly outside strip joints where, inside, bored girls peel their clothes, and the men sit as far from one another as can be managed.

That is Soho. But there is a Soho, or something close

to it, wherever *Hair* is played. It is Forty-second Street, a
few blocks from Broadway. It is San Francisco's Tenderloin,
around the corner from the theaters of Geary Street. It is
Clark Street, west of Chicago's Loop. Like Soho, they are the
festering pimples of an unnatural diet on which society has
been force-fed.

We had it all wrong—most of us, at least. We "learned"
the facts of life from our friends in the street, or from one
paragraph in a Boy Scout handbook entitled "Conservation,"
or occasionally from a book on reproduction self-consciously
thrust in our hands by parents. (Those of us whose parents
talked at all about sex were a minority. A few years ago,
William Blaisdell, a public health specialist of Washington,
D.C., asked a gathering of 624 educators to indicate whether
they had learned about sex first from their parents. Not one
raised his hand.) When we started having girls, they were
the kinds of girls one had, not the kind one married. Until
I married, I had never had intercourse with a woman for
whom I truly cared. Under the circumstances, it was a miracle that any of us managed to fuse love with sex. We were
the lucky ones. For many, many others sex meant—and still
means—frustration, nightmares, even ulcers and other dis-
eases. And for each person emotionally or physically scarred
by sex, there were thousands more for whom it was no more
than a toy, a game, a shallow selfish quest.

The corollary to the burial of sexuality was that feelings
weren't nice. One should suffer in silence. He certainly should
never cry. Emotions were, at best, unreliable and impolite.
Much of the sensory apparatus by which humans communicate feelings to one another was restricted or lost to them. I
remember once hearing a new father asking his doctor until
what age it would be all right for him to kiss his son.

If the Devil himself had conspired to create hell on

earth, he would have started here. People who don't know what it means to feel human cannot comprehend the humanness of others. People cannot respect others when they cannot respect themselves.

When such conditions exist, communication between human beings—the foundation of civilized life—is blocked.

Communication takes many forms. It consists mainly of spoken dialogue. But spoken dialogue can be a deceptive indicator of meaning. It has its own several forms. It can reflect what a person really believes; what he would like you to think he believes; or what *he* would like to think he believes.

To know which of these meanings to apply to words, you must engage in other, nonverbal forms of communication. This kind of communication consists of what you see, standing at the side as a neutral observer; of what you feel, with all your conditioning and biases engaged; of what you deduce that another person is feeling, based on your knowledge and perception of him; and finally of what you imagine you would feel if you were the other person.

Only when you step out of your own traces and into those of another being can you perceive outside your own set of givens. Only then does dialogue—and communication —occur.

Only when communication occurs in such fashion, can a couple experience love.

Only when communication occurs in such fashion can nations, religions, races, or generations understand and accept one another. And that is the point where the political implications of our raucous, threatening, envy-producing sexual revolution begin to come clear.

It is no trick at all to see reality through the eyes of someone whose way of looking at the world corresponds to your own. What is difficult and threatening is to see it through the eyes of someone whose way does not correspond to your own. To accomplish that feat, a man requires sufficient inner strength; in other words, self-respect. But he can never respect himself in a social setting in which he is taught that what he is and feels is base.

Before a man can make what Arthur Schlesinger, Jr., calls "the imaginative leap" into another man's shoes, he must feel solid in his own. That is the very solidity developing today.

Man does tend to accept the social setting he inherits—but only to that point where his frustrations become so painful he can no longer bear them. Then, with an outraged roar, he rebels.

Frustrations produce distortions. Efforts to remove the frustrations produce their own distortions, in turn. So it is only natural that the rebellion against repression would carry to the extremes of sexual expression that characterize the arts—and life itself—today.

These extremes may or may not be valid signs of where we're heading, but they are invaluable in showing us where we've been. The story behind a historic example will help me make my point.

One morning a few years ago, I read a small notice in a French magazine about a new Swedish film. That afternoon, I called my New York office. The next day, I was en route to Stockholm to see the film. I saw it twice, then spent several days talking to the director, his star, and a number of other Swedes who had been directly or indirectly associated with the film. I returned to Paris, wrote the story, and sent it off to New York. A few days later, my editor, Bill Arthur, telephoned me: "Len," he said regretfully, "I'm afraid we're not quite ready for that yet at *Look*." I filed the story away.

One year later, I received a cable from *Look* in New

York. Did I have a copy of the story? *Look* was now ready.

The film, of course, was *I Am Curious (Yellow)*, and the difference was that after a long legal battle, the film had just opened in New York, and lines of people were wrapped around the theaters.

I Am Curious (Yellow) is the story of a young girl who is, or was, curious about politics, nonviolence, Zen, commitment, Socialism, other Swedes, and sex. She is also angry—about Swedes who preach democracy and vacation in Franco's Spain, who vote for a socialist state, but abandon their efforts to achieve it. If *I Am Curious (Yellow)* was tedious, it was also a serious film with a noble theme and, in dramatic terms, original. But the originality that marked it for the average man was of an entirely different sort. To the best knowledge of Sweden's knowledgeable film historians, it was the first movie involving characters more complex than a restless housewife and a wayward milkman to portray explicit acts of sex.

The first sexual scenes are rollicking fun. Imagine Mack Sennett directing sex, and you'd be pretty close. An early morning joust astraddle a balustrade of the Royal Palace, while the sound track plays the Swedish national anthem, qualifies as one of the more outrageously comic moments in film. But the sex soon turns sour, vulgar, selfish, violent. Angered because her lover does not tell her about another woman, the leading lady—who preaches nonviolence as a technique of national defense—finds she cannot honor its principles in personal life. In a dream, she kills and castrates her lover.

The two characters use each other; they do not care about each other—and director Vilgot Sjöman uses sex to make a political point: lack of commitment in affairs of state is as disastrous as in affairs of heart.

This is all very good for politics, but is it good for sex? In one way it is not very good at all. If I were a fifteen-year-old learning about sex through this film, I think I would consecrate my life to baseball. For Sjöman makes something violent and frightening out of what should be serene and affirming.

But for many, many people it isn't and if there is a historical point and value to the film, it lies precisely here. What we are participating in as readers and viewers is a self-confrontation by artists for whom sex has been sad—and who are brave enough to admit it. Art, like news, examines distortion. Couples with fifty years of marital bliss etched into their faces get their picture in the local press. Star-crossed lovers make plays.

Both director Sjöman, and Lena Nyman, his star, emphasize that their part in this movie most definitely derives from their own lives. He is a big, innocent-looking man in his mid-forties, with a beguiling, almost cherubic face and a deliberate manner. "Do you really want people to know that this is the kind of thing you have going on in yourself?" he wondered silently. As a good artist must, he decided he did. Over coffee one day in Stockholm he told me, "The artist has to approach the borders of taboos. He must try to break them in public so he can breach them himself."

Excess is the companion of catharsis. Not for nothing are the scenes of sex without a redeeming moment of beauty. This is not a celebration. It is a war.

Sjöman comes from proletarian, puritan stock. His film, said one Swedish film producer, was "a fist fight with his own puberty." By his own admission, vulgarity shocked and inhibited him, and he could not handle sex.

Miss Nyman's upbringing was not puritanical but it was conventional. She overreacted. "I had sexual experiences too early," she recalled during a long talk we had in her Stockholm apartment one morning. "I threw off restraints too vigorously." When I asked her if the film could have been made in a less explicit style, she replied, "Yes, but not by Vilgot and not with me. I thought at the time, 'We should show the Swedish people love and sex in a natural way.' Now, two years later, I feel I wanted to free myself, not only the Swedish people." Her voice rose now, and she bounced her small fists on the coffee table. "All sorts of conventions are over society. Shadows obscure reality, and I'm against them. If I don't break down conventions and free myself from them, think what they could do to my life. I shall live fifty, sixty years or more. They could make my life dishonest." Convention, she went on, causes people either to restrain themselves unnaturally or to rebel excessively, as was the case with her. In either case, the result is unhappiness. What she and director Sjöman both wanted was an environment in which neither suppression nor rebellion distorted individual choice. And they were willing to go to extremes to make their point. As Sjöman told me: "Through sex, I do reach a tremendous audience. That was one of its functions. If you're speculating with sex and you have nothing to say artistically, you're going to have a bad film. But if you have something to say, you're on safe ground."

Fifteen years ago, a movie actor would collapse into a chair and be fetched a glass of water by his movie wife, who had just announced to him that they were about to have a wee one.

Today, movies grapple with reality as we know it exists.

How had this gap between myth and reality been permitted to exist for so long? Movie critic Richard Shickel

suggests one good answer: As long as there was no competition, movie producers could aim unashamedly at the surefire
twelve- or thirteen-year-old mentality. Television removed
that crutch. To survive, the movie industry had to find an
audience; it aimed itself this time at the educated New Class.

There is perhaps, an additional element to the answer.
Hollywood had imagined it was pandering to public taste:
it mistook the judgments of the churches, the courts, and the
self-appointed watchdogs of public morality as expressions
of the public will. In one generation, this same public will
has annihilated legal and religious restraints against the
rights of artist to express reality as they see it and offer their
works for judgment. In 1949, I smuggled *Tropic of Cancer*
home from Europe. In 1969, it became a film.

Here is an excellent example of how a segment of contemporary history has been telescoped, giving us a false image
of our times.

Because each rupture of our antiquated moral code is
treated with such astonished relish by the press, the atmosphere is charged with a feeling of revolution and moral disorder. One generation, the under-thirties, appears to have
suddenly upended reality. In fact, these breakthroughs in
social acceptance are at the cutting edge of an evolutionary
process that had required more than a generation's time and
managed to touch all of life.

Over the last thirty years, an onslaught of revelations
about human personality has purged puritanical remnants
from many churches, schools, and homes. The negative position toward sexuality exhibited in certain religious institutions has slowly but steadily been replaced by one holding
that sensual pleasure is a gift of God, and that the Bible
proves it. Certain ministers are privately—and in a few cases,
publicly—condoning conduct that generations of Americans

had been conditioned to regard as sinful. Masturbation, for example, is seen as a normal practice that should cause no concern. It does no physical harm; its only danger is the guilt that grows from it through popular misunderstanding of the religious position toward the act.

Various forms of love play, practiced by many people despite church censure, are in certain instances now being viewed as natural expressions of love, perfectly acceptable so long as they are found to be agreeable to the lovers. Sexual deviation is being viewed with infinitely more tolerance. Finally, and most impressively, premarital intercourse is now seen in a radically different light in some religious circles.

Certain Protestant theologians would contend that, biblically, a marriage had always been constituted by just two things—mutual consent plus physical union. They assert that once a man and woman have vowed to remain together and have actually joined together, they are married in God's sight, no matter what their status might be in the church or society. If they have vowed to wed, formally, or otherwise, for as long as they live, their "premarital intercourse" is really not that at all, this view holds. Besides being the deepest expression of their mutual love, physical union is regarded as the very act that makes them one in the eyes of God.

A critically important theology accompanies these changing ideas. It is expressed in different ways by different men, but its gist is approximately this: Man is a unique being created by God. The closest he can come to knowing God is to know as much as he can about God's creation—himself. To fail to know himself fully is to know less than he can of God. Sin is no longer deviation from strict behavioral norms. It is alienation from one's true being.

That is the theological language, as I described it twelve years ago in my book *God and Freud*. Since then, the language has permeated young life. In today's vernacular, it is called "doing your own thing."

Our changing concepts have enabled us to equip children with accurate biological facts through a dialogue that barely existed when I was growing up. (I shall never forget the shock I felt one day in 1965, as I sat in on a fifth-grade sex education class in East St. Louis, Missouri—and realized that I was learning.) But even more to the point, our changing concepts have permitted us to engage in a dialogue with children that alters their most basic feelings of all—about what it means to be human. There is another episode I won't forget in this regard. This is how I described that episode in an article I wrote for *Look:*

The prep school was a New Jersey landmark. The speaker was a grandmother. The topic was sex. "Dr. Mary Calderone," said Headmaster James Howard of Blair Academy, "addresses the subject of sex with greater knowledge than probably almost anybody." For the next 90 minutes, sweet, 61-year-old Dr. Calderone talked to 320 boys as they had never been talked to before.

"People think sex education is when they tell children how babies are born. That's not it. Sex is not reproduction, and it's not coitus, although both are part of it. Sex is what it is to be a man or a woman. What that was before is not what it is today.

"What is sex for? It's for fun, that I know, for wonderful sensations. It's also for reproduction, sedation, reward, punishment. It's a status symbol, a commercial come-on, proof of independence, a form of emotional blackmail. Many of these are negative ways of using sex. What we are trying to feel our way toward are the positive ways. Sex is not something to be feared or degraded or kicked around or used. Sex is not something you turn off like a faucet. If you do, it's unhealthy. We are sexual beings, legitimately so, at every age. Don't think that sex stops at the age of 50. It doesn't.

"We need new values to establish when and how we should have sexual experiences. Nobody's standing on a platform, giving answers. You are moving beyond your parents. But you can't just move economically or educationally. You must move sexually, as well. You must learn how to use sex. This is it: first, to separate yourselves from your parents: second, to establish a male or female role; third, to determine value systems; fourth, to establish your vocational role. Our sex expresses itself in everything we do. Sex," concluded Grandmother Calderone, "is not just something you do in marriage, in bed, in the dark, in one position." As she took her seat, Headmaster Howard left his to lead the boys of Blair in a sustained ovation.

I remember how, when the headmaster called for questions, the school's student leader shot to his feet. "What is your opinion of premarital intercourse among teenagers?" he demanded.

"What's yours?" Mary Calderone shot back. When the uproarious laughter finally ended, she declared, "Nobody on high decides this. You decide it yourself."

That episode and the exchange that followed were destined to become the most abused passages I had ever written.

Some months after my article appeared, Dr. Calderone wrote me a warm letter detailing the immediate, pleasant aftermath. Inquiries had poured in to her New York office from all over the country. She had been invited to address dozens of institutions. One night she went to Washington as the guest of Mrs. Robert McNamara, who had assembled some of Washington's most imposing figures for a dinner discussion. In the course of the evening, Dr. Calderone was able to inform the then U.S. Secretary of Defense that masturbation at West Point was an offense punishable by expulsion. My article, Dr. Calderone assured me, had served the cause of sexual enlightenment in the United States.

Two years later, I received a second letter from Dr. Calderone. Sex education in general, and she, specifically, had come under attack from conservative U.S. elements. The material for the attack had been lifted chiefly from my article.

But the citations had been butchered.

The long opening quotation had been edited by pamphleteers as follows: "What is sex for? It's for fun . . . for wonderful sensations. Sex is not something you turn off like a faucet . . . We need new values to establish when and how we should have sexual experiences." The exchange that followed had been deftly distorted through the addition of a single word. To the question "What is your opinion of premarital sex relations among teenagers?" Dr. Calderone was said to have answered, "What's yours? Nobody from up on high, *God*, determines this . . ." Dr. Calderone never uttered that word. Nor was she, a practicing Christian, denying God. She was simply paraphrasing what she'd said earlier: "Nobody's standing on a platform, giving answers." She was telling the student leader that he must establish values through the process of his own reason; he could not surrender responsibility to some human authority.

The attack on Dr. Calderone illustrates how awesome and frightening individual freedom can be to those not accustomed to it. (". . . man finds his emotional ties to a superior authority, which he blindly obeys . . ."). The attack further illustrates how enlightenment produces an immediate rocker motion of action—reaction. But if I am right, there is a positive element to this illustration that will endure long after the negative ones are forgotten. For Mary Calderone's response to that student answers a much larger question than the one it was meant to serve.

Today, at last, sex *is* what it is to be a man or a woman —which happens to include sexuality. Sex *is* what it means to feel human and self-respecting. Man's self-acceptance is a signal achievement in his quest for freedom with vast social and even political implications that are only now beginning to be considered.

There are those who see such implications in the removal of sex from man's storehouse of repressed feeling—and they make an impressive case.

Sexual fulfillment is richest when it occurs between two equal partners, each possessed of such respect for his own worth that he is capable of the prime act of love—surrender. Until recent years, sex "worked" on a "double standard" that indulged a man and imprisoned a woman. The cultural difference was based on a biological fact. A man who had sexual intercourse risked nothing except the possibility of disease; a woman risked, that, too, but far more to the point, she risked pregnancy and social ostracism.

None of these risks need apply today. Disease is controllable. Contraceptives are vastly improved and widely available, and so are abortions, should a mistake occur. One consequence of these advances was to permit human emotion to achieve a natural level.

The double standard, one for men, another for women, established a competitive base at the very foundation of life. What might happen to a society whose basis of sexual conflict has been removed? No one yet knows, because such a society has never existed before in a modern, highly developed setting. But the question is no longer remote.

Today a technique that did not exist twenty years ago sweeps the psychological landscape. Groups of diverse human beings whose skins and sex and age and orientations may wildly differ enter the arena of fellowship together trying to break down those conventions that keep people distant from one another. The methods to this achievement are multiple and occasionally bizarre. What they share is the idea that risking involvement is the essential psychological transport toward human community. Released feelings, say disciples of this movement, are the trumpets that crumble Jericho fortresses men build to separate people, systems, nations. To restore feelings between them, it is necessary to unblock the emotional walls they have built against one another. Destructive impulses may retain their sexual disguise but appear in some sublimated form as tensions or aggressions between the partners. Somehow, in some way, that aggression has to emerge—either as an emotion directed against other human beings, or as an illness that tears at human tissue.

It would be foolish, indeed, to suggest that all human conflict is rooted in sex and would end if sexual conflicts ended. It would not be foolish at all to suggest that when sexual conflicts diminish, a barrier to understanding is breached.

Surrender is not merely an act of love. It is a requisite to dialogue and understanding as well.

Only when men who have traditionally enclosed their emotions develop the capacity to unblock does the possibility of fellowship arise.

Fellowship. What a tantalizing idea. Many would call it wishful, even pious. Yet it is precisely here where we must look for the ultimate meaning of what passes for the sexual revolution—but is in fact much more.

It is the implications of the attack against outmoded, authoritarian social morality that are so frightening to those with an investment in the past. For once authority has been successfully assailed in one area, other assaults automatically follow.

An orderly society can be heaven on earth if the nature of the order is such that it reflects the desires of its inhabitants and provides a peaceful setting in which they can achieve their potential. An authoritarian society may inhibit potential, suppress instinct, and accumulate such a collection of repressed impulses that discontent erupts in myriad ways.

While freedom of action and expression exist in the United States to a remarkable degree, the expectations of the majority have, until recently, been based on a rigid set of assumptions about conduct, morality, and aspirations.

Newton's law that action produces reaction is as valid for society as it is for physics. The violent attack on traditional values today is in some measure due to the rigidity of a morality that dictated how we should feel and respond, what we should wear and say, and to what objectives we might aspire and work. The only form of aggression that was not proscribed—and in fact was given moral license through the Protestant ethic—was the acquisitive urge.

Here again, the overt character of current events tends to telescope and distort history. Today's sexual rebels—if a group so large and influential can any longer be called rebels —are not the instigators but the *beneficiaries* of a process that started years ago. This process questioned the prevalent sexual morality in the context of a much larger challenge to authority itself.

The outbreaks against social authority today are a direct consequence of new concepts of human relations that have developed over the last thirty years. Derek Miller, clinical professor of psychiatry at the University of Michigan, explains: "As the child grows up more and more parents have tried to conceive of him as an individual with special and unique needs. . . . Children learn in their own family group not only that they themselves have the capacity to make value judgments but that authority figures are often unsure of themselves and often wrong."

The broad attack against authoritarian morality, which goes under the heading of the sexual revolution, is thus far more than just a matter of changing of a sexual code, or even of an attack on authority. It is a breakthrough toward real relationships between human beings.

It is precisely here where the new theology addresses itself to contemporary life by urging that man treat his fellow man not as an object—an "It"—but as a person—a "Thou."

The I—Thou dialogue formulated by the Jewish theologian Martin Buber became the bedrock of a new, man-centered theology that turned a significant portion of organized religion away from ruminations about the afterlife and toward a confrontation with the choices between heaven and hell in the here and now. As one Christian theologian explained it to me in 1959, "Martin Buber brought God to earth."

But Buber went further. He said that God was the biggest circle man could draw around his neighbors.

Is this pious? Is this wishful? Cast your eye across the panorama of "history's largest happening" ten years later, when 400,000 young people extended their arms in a vast circle into which they drew their neighbors.

"The baffling history of mankind is full of obvious turning points and significant events," *Time* Magazine noted in the aftermath of this one, "battles won, treaties signed, rulers elected or deposed, and now, seemingly, planets conquered. Equally important are the great groundswells of popular movements that affect the minds and values of a generation or more, not all of which can be neatly tied to a time and place. Looking back upon the America of the '60s, future historians may well search for the meaning of one such movement. It drew the public's notice on the days and nights of August 15 through 17, 1969, on the 600-acre-farm of Max Yasgur in Bethel, N.Y.

"What took place at Bethel, ostensibly, was the Woodstock Music and Art Fair, which was billed by its youthful Manhattan promoters as an 'Aquarian Exposition' of music and peace. It was that and more—much more. The festival turned out to be history's largest happening. As the moment when the special culture of U.S. youth of the '60's openly displayed its strength, appeal and power, it may well rank as one of the significant political and sociological events of the age.

"What the youth of America—and their observing elders —saw at Bethel was the potential power of a generation that in countless disturbing ways has rejected the traditional values and goals of the U.S. Thousands of young people, who had previously thought of themselves as part of an isolated minority, experienced the euphoric sense of discovering that they are, as the saying goes, what's happening."

One participant summed it up: "People are getting together," he said simply. It was the manner in which they did that stunned the country. There had been dire predictions of wantonness and violence, and indeed, there was an openness about sex and drug-use that made one wonder if one stifling conformity had been decimated only to create another. But these reservations aside, an enduring historical benchmark was built. Said *Time:* "Bethel produced a feeling of friendship, camaraderie and—an overrused phrase—a sense of love among those present. . . . If Bethel was youth on a holiday, it was also a demonstration to the adult world that young people could create a kind of peace in a situation where none should have existed, and that they followed a mysterious inner code of law and order. . . ."

I don't think it's wishful to suggest that Woodstock validates a capacity for encounter that has never existed before to the degree it does today.

Can this capacity for encounter invade our political processes? To an extent, it has already. Our sit-ins, our Marches on Washington, our Moratoriums for Peace, all are expressions of political encounter. But can encounter ever pass from the realm of conflict and confrontation into enduring relationships between men? It can—but only when the time comes that *all* men feel like men.

That simple idea is the key to the complex drama we Americans are acting out today. Many factors produced what Gunnar Myrdal so aptly christened the American Dilemma; many solutions must be applied before the dilemma yields. But all must serve this central idea—that black Americans do not feel like men. Until they do, they cannot relate, not to whites, not even to one another.

They are learning now to feel like men. It is a painful experience for everyone, but absolutely essential. Let us look now at a specific experience, and see what it can produce.

CHAPTER THREE

LEW DOUGLASS
Bedford-Stuyvesant

He was talking about the early '6os, when all the white liberals were suddenly gaga over Negroes, and he chuckled and shook his head: "I could dominate a cocktail party. I could tell them the moon is green and they'd believe me. Sometimes I would say to myself that what I'm saying is STOO–PID."

He shook his head again, a surprisingly pasty-faced head, more a pale gray-brown, round, with a wide nose supporting steel frame glasses, and straight hair. And he laughed again, a gut-bucket chuckle, one short, high "hee" that belonged to a stereotype, not a law-school graduate. It was a testament to his liberation, that chuckle. So was the black quality he gave to his "yeah," higher and more pronounced than mine. What was it he had said just minutes before? "When I went to school, I was more Ivy League than the Ivy League guy. Three-button suits, the whole bit. It was a matter of great pride when someone said on the telephone, 'I didn't know you were a Negro.' We were trying to become dark-skinned Americans. We didn't want to be black."

He had come full circle. He was sitting at a desk now on the nineteenth floor of Brooklyn's Granada Hotel, the

assistant director of the Bedford-Stuyvesant Restoration Corporation, one half of a hydra-headed attempt to mate the
most and least powerful people in America. Bedford-Stuyvesant Restoration Corporation would structure the community's rebuilding program on the basis of local sentiments
and needs. Bedford-Stuyvesant Development and Services
would fund and advise it into reality. Behind Lew Douglass
was a window, and through that window you could see the
wreckage of the district in which he was born. There were
gaping holes now where buildings had been before the historic 1964 riots that had taught America the meaning of
"Burn, baby," and articulated the vocabulary of black rage.
When Lew was born in 1930, the Negro population of Bedford-Stuyvesant was 30,000. Today it pushed 500,000, a re-
pository of every problem, every sin, every crime, every lost
hope and bitter sentiment of America's 30,000,000 poor. It
stood there, collecting dropouts from Harlem, sprawling,
vermin-ridden, hopeless—first an irksome, then a violent,
and finally a flaming contrast to Wall Street just across the
river. Lew had crossed the river to Manhattan to be an
assistant U.S. attorney ("There's always one black U.S. attorney") and now he was back to see whether Wall Street
itself could cross the river and resolve the American dilemma.
Ever since the 1964 riots, everyone had been telling everyone
else how desperate the situation had become; and no help
whatsoever had been forthcoming despite the outburst of
pledges that had followed in the wake of the riots. In February, 1966, bitter black residents turned on Robert Kennedy
at a meeting in Brooklyn that followed his tour of the area.
"I'm weary of study, Senator," Civil Court Judge Thomas
Jones, the community's leading black, told the startled Senator. "Weary of speeches, weary of promises that aren't kept.

. . . The Negro people are angry, Senator, and judge that I am, I'm angry too. No one is helping us."

Kennedy had already determined to try. The month before he had given three speeches on three successive days that had provided a global view of the Negro problem. Kennedy challenged the two favorite remedies of social welfare, relief and public housing. He raised three comparatively new ideas instead. The first was the absolute necessity for creating a sense of community within the slum. The second, which followed from the first, was the need for participation on the part of slum tenants in the decision-making process. The third was the need for private industry to help. The first two ideas had been expressed in enabling legislation for the War on Poverty. The third was Kennedy's alone.

It was out of these ideas that Kennedy's Bedford-Stuyvesant project emerged. After almost a year of study, of jousting with politicians whose lives were more secure when traditional channels of welfare were used, the outlines of the project had been enlarged to include virtually the entire ghetto. There would be a program to create jobs, another to rehabilitate housing, still another to improve health, sanitation, and recreation facilities. Two superblocks would be constructed as models and experiments for others that could hopefully follow. An old, shut-down bottling plant would be fashioned into a community center. The powerful people whose help Kennedy had enlisted would arrange a mortgage consortium to free residents of devastating double and triple high interest payments; they would stump for locating industry in the area. There would even be a university geared to the needs of this community of dropouts.

Many another slum program had died aborning. Kennedy's combined three precious ingredients: it was total; it understood that the slum-dwellers themselves must do the job, not simply to get the job done, but to confirm themselves in the process; and it appealed more powerfully to the white Establishment than any previous project. The Development and Services Corporation had C. Douglas Dillon, former Secretary of the Treasury, for its board chairman; board members included Thomas J. Watson, Jr., of IBM; George S. Moore of First National City Bank; Benno Schmidt of J. H. Whitney; and André Meyer of Lazard Frères. Part of the lure was surely Robert Kennedy; part was just as surely the challenge: could the men who had profited most from the American society extend its benefits to those who had profited the least? One bridge between them was Lew.

For leadership, the project had settled finally on John Doar, a tall, lean Wisconsin Republican with a legend for civil rights heroics. It was Doar who had cooled off two mobs in Mississippi contesting the registration of James Meredith; it was Doar who had tramped the South thereafter as the Justice Department's key civil rights troubleshooter. Doar's selection was as brilliant as it was belated, and it came just in time: Kennedy's Cinderella dream was only a year old when he arrived, but already it was in trouble, the worst kind of trouble, interior trouble—within its ranks, within the minds of each tough, pragmatic staff member. The first executives had set up an all-black organization in Bedford-Stuyvesant to work up projects and an all-white corporation in mid-Manhattan to dole out money. The memory of what this arrangement produced makes one veteran of the experience shudder. "I came over to Bedford-Stuyvesant like a white investor and audited the books to see whether the niggers could handle their money."

From the outset, the setup had rankled Lew. "We couldn't spend ten dollars without sending a voucher over to

Madison Avenue to have it approved. They worked on us like the CIA. You'd call over there and they wouldn't say Bedford-Stuyvesant D & S, they'd give a number, 0202. It was like a secret operation. And it was all whites there, from the secretary right up, and it was a constant clash, because the blacks resented sending reports to guys over there who they thought were not as competent as they were. Because they're white, it always appears as if they're supervisors. You never get a situation where they initiate a problem or a project and it comes to a black guy who reads it and says, 'No, it's lousy.' It was incredible, the relationship between the two staffs. The black guys wouldn't talk to the white guys."

With one stroke, Doar bunkered the doubts. He put both staffs where the action was, in the Bedford-Stuyvesant slums. "You're here to help," he told the white men privately. "You're not reviewers. You're not superior people."

The suspicion was a long time winding down, even in Lew Douglass's mind.

Some months after it went into operation, the Restoration Corporation obtained three buses from the federal government at no cost. The corporation was obliged to insure the vehicles, however, and to Donald Freeman, a white staff member of the Bedford-Stuyvesant project, that cost seemed excessive in terms of the limited use the corporation could make of the buses. So Freeman recommended to his superiors that the buses be returned to the government. When Lew Douglass heard about the recommendation, he charged down the hall to Freeman's office. "Who the hell do you think you are, you white bastard?" Lew raged. "It's just like the old plantation."

Lew remembers the episode with detachment now.

"I yelled and screamed at him and called him a racist and the funny thing about it, he was really right about the buses. But because of the need for me on the black staff to assert my independence, I argued for the buses. We have since sent the buses back, but I didn't even listen to what he had to say."

Some months later, a stockbroker friend of Freeman's called him for guidance. His firm wanted to put qualified black men on the floor of the New York Stock Exchange; could the Bedford-Stuyvesant people help find one? Freeman consulted George Patterson, a black man who ran the project's job development section. Patterson promised to come up with some names. When several weeks passed and Freeman had still not heard, he then consulted other staff members of the project, who offered several suggestions. Freeman thereupon telephoned Patterson for a comparison of the candidates. Instead of a comparison, he got a battle. Now it was Patterson who charged into his office, shouting that Freeman had exceeded his authority. So loud did he shout that everyone on the floor of the Granada Hotel could hear him. Freeman, an obliging, overly tender man, apologized profusely. Finally, Patterson left. A few minutes later, Lew Douglass appeared in the office of the thoroughly shaken Freeman. "Don," he said, "you have something to learn. You've got to learn that there's such a thing as a black bastard."

Two nights after Robert Kennedy died, Don Freeman and Lew Douglass sat the early morning honor guard vigil together at St. Patrick's Cathedral. "I really felt like I was communicating with him, and we weren't talking," Freeman recalls. "There was really nothing to say. I can't really describe it. We were really having a dialogue."

Lew was thirty-eight, a graduate of Brooklyn College and St. John's Law School, most recently an attorney with the

Office of Economic Opportunity. After my first several minutes with him, I wrote in my notes, "Never smiles." That
wasn't true, I'd soon learn, but it was certainly true now.
He regarded me balefully, seriously, a hard listener.

I told him what I was doing—examining areas of conflict to see whether we were at the point of cataclysm or on
the verge of revelation. The white-black dialogue was one
test, and Bedford-Stuyvesant the best case study.

"You want me to react?" he asked. "Okay. This is a new
kind of commitment on the part of the white power brokers.
But it's the same old adherence to traditional attitudes. It's
administered by the same kind of people that do the same
kind of thing in their own corporations. It's got power-struc-
ture echoes. These guys are sayin', 'Since we have our money
involved, we are not going to let it be stolen.' Yet I have to
believe that there's a real moral concrete commitment.
Whether it can be translated to dollars, I don't know.

"I'm still an all-out integrationist. I don't think we're
going to make separate communities. The common level
ought to be economic, not racial. The answer is to make the
kids in Bedford-Stuyvesant feel that they belong to the American system.

"America is a good place to be. It's a pleasant life. Our
people want to be part of it—but be black and be part of
it. We have to give back identity to the Negroes. After they
get this pride back, they can be more effective. When they're
aggressive, they can deal on even terms."

He'd been cultivating two new habits, he told me. The
first was to write down the name of every person he met. The
second was to Xerox everything he came across in his reading
that seemed pertinent to the black dilemma. From *Crisis in
Black and White,* he had Xeroxed a portion of Chapter VII
that contained these words:

By itself . . . all the race pride in the world will not solve the Negro's crisis of identity. In the last analysis, what Negroes need more than anything else is to be treated like men—to believe, in their hearts, that they *are* men, men who can stand on their own feet and control their own destinies. . . .

. . . self-hate stems more from Negroes' unequal position relative to power than from any lack of knowledge of self. . . . Thus the principal solution to the problem of Negro personality and identity is the acquisition of power: political, social and economic.

The other reprint was from *Black Rage,* by William H. Grier and Price M. Cobbs, two black psychiatrists, a book of rare insight. Chapter Ten deals with Malcolm X; the pages Lew now offered me made a point that would become thematic in my subsequent days in Bedford-Stuyvesant. Admiration for Malcolm within the black community subsequent to his death had formed the philosophical basis for black activism, the authors wrote. But, unlike the man who inspired them, the black militants were static men who "remained encased within the ideas of revolution and black nationhood, ideas Malcolm had outgrown by the time of his death." Ironically, there were men who now found themselves "willing to die for words which in retrospect are only milestones in the growth of a fantastic man."

The authors went on:

Many black men who today preach blackness seem headed blindly toward self-destruction, uncritical of anything "black" and damning white men for diabolical wickedness. . . . Black power activism—thrust by default temporarily at the head of a powerful movement—is a conception that contributes in a significant way to the strength and unity of that movement but is unable to provide the mature vision for the mighty works ahead. It will pass and leave black people prouder, stronger, more determined, but in need of grander princes with clearer vision.

"I'm not at all distressed," Lew was saying now. "The U.S. is better for me certainly than a year ago. I'm not distressed by the problem. We're focusing on the problem. We're getting people involved here who weren't involved before. The people who built Standard Oil of New Jersey and IBM—that kind of talent can be used to develop the city. If we can motivate them we can solve the problem."

Lew apologized then, explaining that he had to see a man from the J. C. Penney Company. The man came in; he was young, and quietly dressed in browns. He explained to Lew that the president of J. C. Penney had proposed in an address at California's San Jose State College that the company and the college "explore the opportunity" of creating some kind of economic development in the San Jose area. A manufacturing product? A service business? The college and its students, he proposed, should take a good look at the needs of the area, with its heavy Mexican-American population. The college, in response, had released an assistant professor for full-time study of this project. Meanwhile, the Penney representative had been touring the country to learn what experiences others had had in the field. "We're just getting underway. We're just getting underway," he kept saying. "These folks have a tremendous talent that has never been allowed to surface."

Lew nodded. It was his turn now. "All over the country major businesses that we now call the private sector and we used to call the power structure are getting involved in problems of minorities. The question is, how best to get the power brokers involved." If he or the J. C. Penney man noticed the instant lapse back to earlier language, neither acknowledged it. "Here's how we do it," Lew said. He explained the setup in Bedford-Stuyvesant, and then stressed its double purpose, first, to create black-owned businesses, second, to encourage major firms to move into ghetto areas.

"Whatever you do is only going to be successful if you get the community involved at the outset. What we resent most of all is that someone else is going to program our lives."

He told the Penney man how, with his company's presence lending legitimacy in the eyes of government and institutions, they could create a community group that in turn could create low-cost housing.

"You're going to have flak," Lew warned. "Suppose we want to build a Black Panther School? You're not going to agree with that, but those are the things you would have to work out." Then he asked his visitor:

"Does J. P. Penney issue franchises?"

The visitor's finger shot out at Lew. "C. Penney," he said.

"Does J. C. Penney issue franchises?"

"We don't, but our eyes aren't closed to it."

The appeal needn't always be moral, Lew stressed. He mentioned one tire manufacturer whom they had approached to set up a black franchise. "I don't care anything about civil rights, philanthropy, or charity," the manufacturer said bluntly. "All I know is we get a profit every time we sell a tire." They got the franchise.

"Once you make a decision to get involved, you should realize you're going to have problems. All the black people don't agree with each other. We not only fight for the programs, we fight about them. Commitment means that Penney's going to have to take a little heat. It may get picketed. Commitment means letting the poor people decide and make mistakes. You can't say to them, 'You can make decisions,' and later say, 'Not *that* decision!' "

He told the Penney man then about a new systems

manufacturing plant IBM had installed in an abandoned, cavernous bank building. Most of the new employees had been drawn from within 1½ miles of the plant. The company had not disqualified anyone because of a criminal record or lack of high-school diploma. The management staff was fully integrated. Two little restaurants had opened alongside the plant. All clearing and restoration contracts had been awarded to blacks. That was the kind of thing the black community wanted, Lew said. He saw no point to the involvement of San Jose State; the college would take two years and come up with a study. They didn't need more studies. "Everybody knows the problems. What we need are the J. P. Penneys to come in with the money."

The man from J. C. Penney did not flinch.

Then Lew offered a concrete way in which Penney could do good for the minority and itself.

"If J. P. Penney could set up a supplier . . ." he mused. The company could exercise an informal influence over the supplier's management requirements, simply by being the major market for the supplier. That was the idea: Penney would be the chief recipient of the product. "This guy could supply Penney with something—and go out and look for other business," Lew explained. The Penney man nodded; his eyes never left Lew's face. Locate the man in the ghetto, Lew stressed, and let him find his business elsewhere. Or, when the time comes to put up shopping centers in the ghettos, let the blacks or Mexicans own small stores in those centers. Unless minority participation and ownership were an integral part of the operation from the outset, the radicals would think it was a scheme on the part of the power struc- ture to recapture the city.

The man kept nodding.

"Can I write your name down?" Lew said. "I decided

I'm going to remember names." The man gave him a card and while Lew was writing his name down, the man said, "We had to learn how to merchandise to you folks, to give you real leather coats and not fake leather coats."

If Lew heard what the man said, he did not let him know it. Instead, he went on, "Just creating jobs isn't the answer because all the black people were working before 1865. Don't forget to get involved with some of the local communities. If you get involved with the poor, they're going to come up with the same conclusion you do. They may even be more conservative than you if you get them involved enough." He told his visitor how IBM had asked militants and separatists to come up with a screening program. IBM gave $2,500 for a study, which was done by a member of Sonny's Carson's Black Panthers. When Lew saw the program he thought its standards were too high. But when he objected, he was told off by the people who did the study. "Don't give me nothin'," one said. "That's my trainin' program."

The Penney man thanked him and left. Lew shrugged. "I could ask this guy 'How many black managers or Mexican managers you got?' and throw him in a state of depression. But I don't. He means well."

"How do you feel when he says 'You people?' "

"I flinch, because I grew up in that time when it was a derogatory phrase."

Lew Douglass's father grew up in Brooklyn. He did not finish high school. Lew's mother graduated near the top of her class at Girls' High. She attended Brooklyn College for three years, then moved through a series of civil service jobs.

When the Douglass family moved uptown it was not to break the color barrier, simply to secure better housing.

Those whites still living on his new block sold their homes
to blacks and left.

In those days, black parents did not speak about color
in front of their children. "I found out that I was a Negro
when my friend, who was five years old, told me he was
white. I just remember being really disappointed in not
being what he was," Lew said.

"My parents took what was then the Negro liberal
position, supporting the NAACP. I've talked about the psychological damage. I don't know if that happened in my
family. The other day, my mother read *Black Rage* and she
said to me, 'I never thought when I grew up that everything
was colored by the fact that you're Negro. I don't remember
that being in my experience. Was that part of your experience?' And my answer was yes.

"I can remember being in junior high school and getting
so mad at a teacher. In '43, there were some race riots in
Harlem. I can visualize that woman now, a young, pretty
woman from Texas. She said that there was no problem in
the South because the Negroes and the white people loved
each other, and she could remember going to the porch of
the woman who was her nanny or maid or something and
drinking lemonade in the evening and how comfortable and
pleasant it was. And I remember becoming so enraged because she didn't understand how demeaning it was to go
over there and drink in this woman's shack. And I remember sitting in the back of the class and I wanted to get
up and say something, you know, but at the time—we're
talking '44, '43—Negro kids didn't get up and talk about
being militant, I mean you were just embarrassed. I remember how I wanted to say something. But I didn't say anything
and I wouldn't have said anything. We had two other Negroes
in the class and they didn't say anything, none of us said any-

thing. We just wanted that woman to stop talking about Negroes and just go on to talk about something else." Lew shook his head. "I still remember that bitch," he said softly.

"And then I had a friend, Ricky. Ricky was a natural leader, best ball player, scholarship to Michigan, he was president of everything. Went into Brooklyn Tech a delinquent. They thought he wouldn't pass school but any time he would take these aptitude tests, he'd score so high they'd say he was a genius. And Ricky described this poem that they read in Brooklyn Tech about Negroes beating on drums and shooting crap, and Ricky put his head down on the desk and tears came to his eyes. And then this little Jewish kid got up —I'll tell you the truth, it was always the Jews that seemed to get up—and said, 'I don't think Negroes are like that,' and Ricky, the toughest kid in the class, he said to me that from then on he was going to protect this kid, that he loved him so because he came to his defense.

"A lot of things happen to you for being black and you kind of forget them. I remember once we were in junior high school and we drew cartoons of each person in class graduating from the ninth grade and they drew a picture of me dressed up in a grass skirt looking at a toothbrush with a light over my head like, you know, I didn't understand what a toothbrush was. The other black guy, they drew as a bellhop and the black girl they drew as an Aunt Jemima. And the thing that was bad is that we laughed. We were mad as hell, but for some reason we were unwilling to display any anger. And I remember one of the real bad gang leaders came over—I was in the rapid advance class, you know, and this real bad gang leader was in the lowest class—and he'd heard about the book and he came over to me and asked should he straighten this shit out. I remember how close I felt to him. He was a delinquent, a really bad guy. Yet I remember that kindred spirit I felt then, that he had heard about this bad situation and he wanted to straighten it out, but at the time I wouldn't resort to going his road. In junior high school, when I was in class with white kids, I just didn't want the subject raised."

Ironically, it was white liberals at Brooklyn College who first roused Lew Douglass to an activist's role. "Hell, they would push us. Sometimes we didn't know we had been insulted. They were really hell raisers. They came to the social affairs in the black community. You felt you could talk about the problems. I never talked about it in mixed groups anywhere else until I got to Brooklyn College."

Then Lew enrolled at St. John's Law School. There were two blacks in his class. "The first conversation in a cafeteria, a guy told me that Negroes, communists, and homosexuals are outcasts, that's a fact of life. I had one white friend. He had an Irish background. He used to tell me crazy stories, like he didn't know the blood of people could be interchanged. I'll tell you the truth, I was very distressed about Catholic education in the United States. I had never seen such a rigid, conservative institution in my life. I went to St. John's because I said, well, I'd been hanging out with Jews all my life so I'll try something else. At Brooklyn College they went out of their way to include a black man in activities and they forced him to become something in the student government. At St. John's I had to force myself to talk about race relations. The majority of the people were right-wing conservative. It was the McCarthy era, and they all supported McCarthy."

Lew graduated law school in 1956. He married, took a job with the rent commission as a hearing officer, and opened a storefront office on Ocean Avenue. As young attorneys have always done, he immersed himself in local Bed-

ford-Stuyvesant affairs. "I was a democratic clubhouse cap-
tain, I was the treasurer and vice-president of the local
NAACP, manager of the Little League, because it's the way
lawyers advertise, in effect." Several years later, he was appointed an assistant U.S. attorney. Then followed jobs with
the Interstate Commerce Commission, and later, the Office
of Economic Opportunity. During all this time, the Doug-
lasses had remained in Bedford-Stuyvesant, but now, like
many American families with children, they found themselves
confronted with a school problem. They asked themselves
whether, to solve it, they should leave Bedford-Stuyvesant for
a white suburb. They decided they would. After some investigation, they chose Hastings-on-Hudson.

The first broker they went to could not have been more
helpful. Not only did he tell them that he tried to encourage
the movement of Negroes into the community, he even offered
to sell them his own house. Of the four brokers the Doug-
lasses contacted, three were helpful. They reported the fourth
to the Fair Housing Commission.

Finally, they found a house they liked, and made an
offer. The owner accepted it. "I don't know whether the
owner said, 'I'm a good person and I'm going to do this,'
or 'I'm getting a good price and I'm going to do this,'" Lew
reflected. In any event, they were soon installed, and almost
instantly and uniformly well received. The exception was
the family across the street, which thought real estate values
would drop.

"I know there are a lot of problems," Lew reflected
now. "I've talked to the militants. The banks discriminate.
But I think by and large they're good people. One neighbor
volunteers to work in Harlem; his kids are in my house every
day. One guy on the corner, he was so friendly he drove me
out of my mind. I had to sneak into the house." Lew laughed.

"Today it's fashionable for everybody to kick the white
liberals. But we wouldn't be where we are if it wasn't for
them. Ten years ago, if the kids came in, the mother and
father would say. 'Sh! The kids don't know yet.' And now!"

Lew had agreed to take me on a tour of his old
neighborhood. Now we took the elevator downstairs and
walked outside to the icy street glaring in the sun. One sweep
of the eye took in the litter of a society that had failed—
boarded windows, broken windows, glass strewn on the street,
empty lots, papers blowing everywhere. We settled into Lew's
car. He pulled into the traffic and headed for the center of
the district. Then he drove east, down one of the main
thoroughfares. Up ahead a tall and skinny black man danced
across the street to a Cadillac parked at the curb. There was
not quite so much litter now. Each block we passed seemed
a little better than the rest. Soon we were on a quiet residen-
tial block where a neighborhood association had posted signs
every few hundred feet. "Watch Your Language, Please," said
one. "Let's Be Neighbors by Showing It," said another. It had
once been a neighborhood of middle-class whites; now it was
all black. In the center of one block stood a three-story
brownstone, merged in with the others, with a small neat
sign that said, "Lewis L. Douglass, attorney." Lew laughed.
"My mother wouldn't take the shingle down after we moved
away." He laughed again, that high, unselfconscious "hee,"
as he told about his mother's reaction to a new job he would
soon be taking in Washington. "You listen to her describe it,
you'd think I was running America."

"What did you call yourself, "Negro" or "black"?" I
asked Lew. Once again we were seated in his office, and he
was remembering.

"We called ourselves "Negro." We were offended when

people used the word "colored." We never used the word "black." I think there was some conscious or unconscious shame about being black. I think that "Negro," by definition, meant a second-rate human being, not only a second-rate citizen. I think that, psychologically, a lot of Negroes in my age group, when they were young, were really ashamed of being Negroes, although this was not something they could verbalize. I know when I was a kid, if a Negro was on radio and made a slip in grammar, I wanted to dive under the desk, I would be so embarrassed. In those days when we used the word "integration" we were really talking about assimilation. I think that we just wanted to get away from the black identity. I remember going to college. We wanted to be Ivy League college types. We called ourselves school boys. I can even remember when I was seventeen or eighteen, there was such a need to show that we were part of the American college scene that even guys that weren't currently enrolled in school would walk around with textbooks, so that people would think they were. Even in the civil rights movement, we would measure the success of a meeting or a protest by the number of white people that were involved. You put together a new organization, you'd say, 'Gee, it's really together, half of it is white.' And the funny thing is, that I really thought in '48 and '50 that we had the answer. I remember going to the March in Washington. That was the most emotional experience of my life. And now, thinking back, I was so happy that I saw a lot of white people, a lot of important white people. That was one of the things that made me think it was so great.

"Some of the things that we did to bring about integration were so artificial. When we were in Brooklyn College, all the Negro kids sat at three tables in the cafeteria, because we were all from Bedford-Stuyvesant or Harlem. I was in a

Negro fraternity, Sigma. Because our social life was segregated, we congregated at these three tables. And every month
we would go through the same thing about, well, this is
artificial segregation, and we would get guys who had some
kind of leadership position and who could stand at each door
of the cafeteria. And each of these guys would always have
a white guy with him. We didn't do anything without that
white liberal being there. And as you came in, he would say,
'You sit on this side of the table,' trying to get the Negro
students dispersed through the cafeteria. But it never worked.
There was this natural need to come together because we
hung out socially.

"I don't know if Negroes have really accepted themselves
yet, but I don't think that the kids in school now would
concern themselves about sitting at separate tables. There is
a pride now about being with other brothers, and letting
that brother know 'I'm with you.' I don't think the thrust
any longer is to disappear.

"It's kind of hard to pinpoint when the change came
about. I know that Malcolm X had a lot to do with it. When
he got started, most of the college crowd, middle-class Negroes
anyway, we kind of laughed at it in the beginning. But the
guy was so smart, and he seemed to win all the debates. After
awhile, people took a lot of pride in what Malcolm was saying. We really liked to see him sock it to 'em on radio and
television, and then, as he began to refine his thinking, then
it was logic, and it became very valid. And I think that he
contributed a lot to the new willingness to be identified as
blacks in America. And then the whole Black Power movement came along, and then the old-line integrationists began
to accept the need not to project integration as the goal, but
to project the need for black people to acquire power so that
you can exercise the options to integrate. When I was in

school, I thought that we were so right, and now it seems so wrong, I can't understand how I could have accepted all of that. But in '48, '50, even '56, I never had the option of saying that I wanted to live in a black community, or that I didn't want to integrate it. Integration became a faith. I can remember picking up an *Ebony* and reading about one Negro vice-president of some big corporation. Boy, I really thought, 'Wow, what a big step, we got this guy as a vice-president,' and I would feel that's a great company. And I never thought about the fact that maybe they had 50,000 white employees and here was this guy sittin' out front. I don't even know if in those days we even thought about black people, to tell you the truth.

"And now, we are talking about what's going to happen to the poor black people. I think it was that integration didn't work. It worked for the successful guys, but when you looked around, statistically it was not working. We went through the whole thing here in New York City, trying to bus the kids back and forth to schools. I was in that fight; I supported those boycotts 100 percent. I said 'integrate the schools,' and I still think that integration probably is the best way to raise the level of education. But now, it's clearer, the cold fact is that we are not going to be able to integrate the school population of New York City. So that, even though emotionally and philosophically I want to see America become an integrated society of black and white people living together, I know that's not going to happen. So I'm going to have to compromise and say, 'Well, let's make these separate black enclaves as good a place to live as possible.'

"At the height of the civil rights movement, the sole objective was to integrate Negroes in the mainstream of American society. That's what we always said. So that if you got one black guy in a plant, you moved forward. If you bought one house in Levittown, you moved forward, and you celebrated that as a great step. We weren't thinking about increasing the strength and the power of the black community. We were really talking in terms of diluting that black community. We weren't going to get integration, we can see now, we were just physically going to locate that black family in that white town, and were physically going to put this black guy in that plant.

"Integration is right and should happen. A lot of this black consciousness is artificial. In the back of my mind I still want to integrate society. But I have concluded that I can't achieve that unless I go through this black bag.

"There are two kinds of separatism. There is the separatism that comes from 'Well, integration hasn't worked, and there are going to be separate black institutions and communities and we have to develop our own identity.' Integration may come about as a consequence. Good. There is nothing wrong with having white friends. There is nothing wrong in becoming involved with the white society. And it may be a good thing in the long run. Then there are separatists who verbalize the concept that the white society is a total evil and we should affirmatively disengage. It's important to have them, because they generate a kind of pride and a kind of integrity, but I don't think that view, in the long run, is going to prevail.

"You go to college campuses and white radicals tell you how American society is sick. They may be right. But to me, it looks very attractive. You put that guy from Bedford-Stuyvesant in business, and he ends up a successful businessman, that guy is gonna want to reach out and get the good things that America has to offer. You can give him all kinds of intellectual explanations, but that guy is still going to want to send his kids to the best schools, wherever they are, he is going to live in an air-conditioned house, he's going to want all the comfort that America has. And when he becomes a successful businessman, he is going to seek to integrate, to seek to get the good things. And I think then he'll begin to relate to white people."

In a few weeks, Lew would be moving to Washington to be the deputy director of the nonprofit housing center of Urban America, a community development corporation. Urban America, established in February, 1965, supplied money for startup costs to community groups that organized to do something about their cities. He would be the first black executive on the staff. And he had some ideas about why he'd been chosen.

"Now the individuals involved in that decision are good people and when they said, "Gee, we ought to get a black guy in here,' that was a good moral decision on their part. But when I work for Urban America, I'm still going to be working within a white segregated structure. And I don't want to make it sound as if this foundation or Ford Foundation or any of the foundations have discharged their responsibilities just by giving me one of their top jobs. They ought to hire more.

"The problem is that these foundations who are thinking about how we restructure cities, they're doing their thinking without including large numbers of black people. So for them to say that 'we have one out of five,' or 'one out of two' is not really the answer, because their whole activity is concerning the lives of black people.

"And when I take the job with Urban America, I'm always concerned that people may think I'm under the impression that they hired me because I'm a smart guy. They've hired me not because of my particular skills or talent but because of the pressure that's been generated from the guys

we call the black militants. And I just want to make it clear
that I understand my responsibilities to the guys on the
street. Because there was a time, you know, when I was at
high school and college, that when a Negro got an important
job, I mean that guy was so jealous about his position, hell,
he wasn't worried about anybody else. If a guy got a job with
a commission or something in the city, you wouldn't see that
guy at a NAACP meeting. He was so worried about his
position that he'd say 'Look, don't hurt me, I've made it.'

"I think I understand why people do things. I can organize and put together the right combinations. Some of us
have to bridge the gap between the Establishment and the
militants. But I wouldn't want to suggest somehow that I'm
better than the guys on the street. I'm no more moral than
anyone else, but I think I have some commitment to help
them with their thing. I'd like to take care of my family and
make a lot of money, but I like to be able to say that I helped
a little bit. I would stay involved only because of this kind
of obligation that I feel. The way the world is structured—
and I don't like this—but those guys are always going to need
me to be the link between them and the Establishment. I
mean, I can deal with the Establishment, because I know how
to fix Martinis."

One of Lew Douglass's last duties before he went to his
new job in Washington was to attend a small luncheon at an
important Brooklyn bank. The meeting had been requested
by the bank, to discuss means in which it might assist in
reviving the community. After some negotiation, and a promise that I would use no names, the bank's officers had invited me to sit in.

"Why are the banks interested?" Lew asked his host.
The answer was that everybody saw the need to rehabili-

tate the city. They were on choice land, with proximity to everything, and it was being abandoned. The city was decaying at the core.

"This is an unusual meeting," Lew said. "The bank is asking, 'What can we do in the ghetto?' Twenty years ago this wouldn't have happened."

The fat man across the table shrugged his shoulders. "If the banks don't find an answer, who's going to? The government. It's become a matter of political philosophy. Do we want more and more government intervention in our lives?" He launched into a big speech then for private enterprise, and there was a simple, theoretical beauty to what he was saying, that industry could do the job better, that it was more efficient, more responsible, cared more about the money it spent, that the quality came out better, that blandness went along with public housing programs, that, in the last analysis, it was almost cheaper to give the money away in interest-free loans than to enlarge housing authorities to a point where tax burdens would become unbearable, that the question, ultimately, was whether to keep the System going or not.

So it had come to this, that one could sit in the dining room of a big Brooklyn bank where the man had sat for years and years indifferent to what was crumbling around him; but now he had thought, and now he could talk about how 1,500 new jobs might cost the government $3 million in support for training and subsidies, but that ultimately the government would get the money back in taxes on the profits amassed by people working profitably who couldn't before. He could talk as they talk now in underdeveloped countries where they try to sell capitalism, these good men, really, representing Sears and Esso and the American chemical companies, and they can show how every job they create may create two more, and how the revenues they generate help support a good share of a country's budget. And how many times I had heard this conversation in many parts of the world, and now, at last, I was hearing it in my own country, just across the river from Wall Street.

And let the disbelievers cry all they will. Economically, it's true. Investment does multiply its effects; it does create more jobs in its wake, as well as tax revenues that can be applied to the social welfare in the form of schools, hospitals, roads, and recreation. The theory is splendid and the execution has been miserable and now at last, perhaps, the frenzy has been such that the American business community will recognize the threat, and wake up and do it.

"As Lenny was saying the other day, the extremes manage to push society more and more toward the middle," Lew said now. And the fat man nodded his agreement to that.

What I'd actually said was that this mass gathering at the middle was constantly being nudged leftward.

CHAPTER FOUR

NUDGING LEFTWARD

I grew up in Chicago in the 1930s in a neighborhood, it was said, that was passing "from Conn to Cohn to coon." People were just beginning to tremble about the last passing when I lived there; South Side Jews were literally being pushed to the edge of Lake Michigan by the slow encroachment of blacks. There was tolerance then, but neither understanding nor compassion on the part of the white population. Our grown-up whites reacted with amused condescension at the riotous night in Chicago's Black Belt when Joe Louis won the heavyweight championship by knocking out Joe Braddock and black men and women poured from their homes and danced down the streets and sang over and over and over again, "Ah told you so, ah told you so." Yes, there was tolerance, amusement, and even an occasional foray to the edges of the ghetto on the west side of Washington Park where one ate fried shrimp and barbecued chicken and speculated about the sexual mystique of blacks. Somehow, in all this process, an idea passed osmotically to us at an early age; one day, when we were playing baseball in Washington Park and saw four black boys start across the park in our direction, thirty of us mounted our bicycles and fled.

I recall another time, many years later, when I brought my family back from Brazil to Manhattan, and enrolled our children in public school. One evening, Linden told us that a classmate had brought several white mice to school, and asked whether she might adopt one. The burden of discouraging her fell to me.

I said that we often went away on trips and that there would be a problem about caring for the mouse. She said that in such an event, she would give the mouse to a friend.

I said that my mother, who had a phobia about mice, would be uncomfortable when she came to our home. She said she would hide the mouse.

I worked my way one by one through every conceivable argument against this mouse; she demolished each in turn. Throughout the dialogue, Jeff was uncharacteristically silent. Finally, exhausted of logic, I confessed to emotion. "The truth of it is, Linden, I just don't like mice," I said at last— at which point Jeff cried, "That's as bad as hating Negroes."

The headlines speak of hatred and violence, but no calculation has yet been made of the moral impact on thoughtful Americans of the racial struggle in the last twenty years. I know that I did not feel as keenly at their age what my children feel today. I know, as well, that their feelings at that earlier age could have derived only from my own. And I like to think that the difference between what passed to me when I was a child and what has passed to them tells something about what has passed in America in that time.

No dates or benchmarks chart this spiritual transition. It was, for the most part, a private event undertaken by a generation weaned in the Depression, jostled by war, and so affected by both that it was more disposed to listen than speak.

I am not comparing darkness and light. The adults I knew believed all the right things. But they did precious little about them. The principles my parents taught me were good ones, and they powered me to occasional honorable acts. At my high-school graduation, I gave one of the class orations —an outraged cry against bigotry hurled at the ears of bigots. In college, I cultivated blacks. But I don't think I understood blacks any better at the time than they understood themselves. And I did not take the kinds of risks and make the kinds of sacrifices that are taken and made today.

"Younger people are willing to walk away from profitable careers to fight a fight they think if not fought would destroy everything we've got here," Donald Freeman, Lew Douglass's Bedford-Stuyvesant colleague, told me one day. "Most of my young friends are involved in this. I think it could be the beginning. Young people won't let it stop. Blacks won't let it stop." Would he? "No. I'll fight for it."

There is no way of making that last sentence not sound precious. Yet, if Donald Freeman is indulging himself, it is in a new kind of American romanticism of which he now constructs his life. The son of affluent New York parents, he attended the University of North Carolina, where panty raids were, in his words, "the most significant thing we did." He graduated an economic conservative who voted for Dwight D. Eisenhower and made a great deal of money, rather quickly, in the construction business, first in Norfolk, Virginia, later in Washington, D.C.

In Washington both his politics and life style underwent substantial change. He tired of building. He felt that making money was not the most satisfying objective in life.

One night, Adam Walinsky, Robert Kennedy's young aide, asked him, "What do you think of setting up a corporation with the most powerful people in the world on one side and Harlem on the other?" Harlem ultimately proved unworkable, but Freeman was caught up in the concept from the outset. When the opportunity to return to New York and work for the Bedford-Stuyvesant group arose, he took it.

Balding, stout, he lives with his wife and two children on a high floor at 450 West End Avenue. The living room is a song of color assembled around new furniture and a big piece of modern marble statuary. He admits readily that he cannot live on his $16,000 a year D & S salary, and knew he couldn't when he took the job. "A lot of us have independent income. None of us live on our salary."

I knew he was right. We'd moved to Europe only a few years earlier from that very neighborhood. It was an uncertain place, once beautiful, now hesitating in that shabby abyss between evacuation by the affluent and restoration by the middle and upper middle class. In the void between need and action one found dope pushers and users along Broadway, perverts in Riverside Park after dark, and thieves probing the area for soft spots. Speculators turned worn-down apartment buildings into cheap transient hotels. Blacks and Puerto Ricans swooped into those lateral streets that sunk fastest, bringing with them the flotsam of human failure. New York's West Side was at once the worst and best neighborhood in America. Living there was a risky, dirty, expensive business, but it meant being engaged somehow with the American dilemma. Already, one could see the physical beginning of resurgence. Lincoln Center had brought life back to the 50s and 60s, urban renewal was restoring a 20-square block area in the 80s and 90s, and young couples were converting brownstones for a chance to live where the action was. All through the area whites and blacks were moving in next door to one another because that was what they wanted. They believed their children should learn through living that that was the right way to live. It was a small commitment to the democratic theory, but a commitment, nonetheless.

We are familiar by now with the heroic expressions of white commitment that characterized the early '6os—the participation in freedom marches and voter-registration drives in the face of threats and actual violence. The headlines report these episodes, but they rarely tell the story of black radicals and white moderates in cities throughout the U.S. working together to bank the summer flames, or of corporate executives in New York, Pittsburgh, Detroit, and elsewhere rousing themselves to live the ideals they have lip-serviced, or of young go-getters ingeniously marrying profit to progress.

They met in a vaulted restaurant just off Wall Street, two young men, one a blue blood, the other Brooklyn-born. At twenty-nine, the blue blood, whose great-grandfather built the Great Northern Rail Road, just might have been that single American at that moment doing more, more concretely and creatively, than any other to reduce the inequities between blacks and whites. At thirty-three, the ex-Brooklynite, whose father never earned more than $100 a week, was a partner in a tiny Wall Street underwriting firm of which stockbrokers spoke with awe; men who invested with him had been known to double their money in a day, multiply it twelve times in four years. A shared streak of impatience had brought the two young men together. As their conversation built, the odds rose to infinity that none quite like it had ever occurred before.

"My idea was to take the greed of people who like to buy stocks and underwrite an issue of ghetto investments," said the broker. But when he'd tried his idea out on the first team of officers at the Bedford-Stuyvesant Project, he'd been completely ignored. Then a third party had told him about Sam Beard.

Beard nodded appreciatively. "*I* deal with the greed line,

too," he said. "People are interested in maximizing profits. If you can get profit and social development to coincide, people are happy to do it."

Six months earlier, Beard explained, he and thirteen other investors had formed a limited partnership worth $400,000 which they'd invested in "go-go" common stocks—stocks with high risk but enormous potential. At the same time, he set up a foundation, called Capital Formation. While the investing partners could pocket their profits, it was their intention to donate the profits to the foundation for use in the ghetto.

Selfless philanthropy? Not precisely. The investors *were* risking their money (a provision of the partnership shuts it down if assets fall to 80 percent of initial value.) But every realized profit would give them a tax deduction.

Now the broker nodded appreciatively.

In its first three months, Beard continued, the partnership's value increased 25 percent. During the same period, Beard marshaled 266 volunteers—many of them friends and former classmates now working for America's leading legal and financial institutions—to enter the ghetto and examine small, mired minority-owned businesses. The foundation then provided blacks and Puerto Ricans with capital donated by the partnership.

Beard laughed. "We talk in terms of our loan committee —which is really me on the telephone. The guy I'm working with says, 'It looks good to me,' so I say, 'Go ahead and do it.'"

Sometimes small sums had worked small wonders. In 1965, an ambitious young black metalworker from East Harlem named Max Josef had quit his foreman's job to set up shop for himself, parlayed a $3,000 investment into an $80,000-a-year lamp manufacturing business. By 1968, he found himself with $20,000 in orders he couldn't fill, so he applied to the banks for a $15,000 expansion loan. No takers. Josef had once cosigned a $1,000 loan on which a friend had defaulted.

A white man in the same bind and circumstances could easily obtain a loan, Beard decided. He sent a financial specialist to Josef. "His attributes are exactly those the financial community beats its brains out looking for every day," the specialist reported. The foundation paid off the debt, and Josef got his loan.

In three months, the foundation had assisted 152 minority-owned businesses, Beard reported. Who could calculate the human profit? He told the story of a young Wall Street banker he'd asked to look into a small metal parts manufacturing shop in Brooklyn, whose Puerto Rican owner had $12,000 in orders, $45,000 in assets, and no prospects of a loan. Though the young banker worked on Wall Street, he had never been to Brooklyn. He did not know how to get there by subway, and because of the stories he'd heard, he was afraid to use his car. So he rented one to cross the river. He inspected the company, recommended a loan—and had returned many times since to help the owner.

"Once you get people involved in something tangible, all the myths disappear," Beard said.

The broker nodded emphatically. "I believe in working through the System, not outside the System."

"We're doing just what you say," Beard said. "We're working within the System."

"I'm good at raising money," the broker mused. "There's a lot of money around. I'm uniquely fitted to do that. I'd be no good over in Bedford-Stuyvesant . . ."

"You wouldn't have to be," Beard said. Could the broker organize another investment partnership, profits from which might be donated to Beard's foundation? Could he get "ten guys who needed the tax deduction to put up $100,000 apiece?"

The broker thought he could. "There are lots of guys who, if approached, would be tickled to death to put you into their hot issues," he said. "Just get someone to write down on a single piece of paper what the tax gimmick is."

As they ate their fish, the two young men compared notes on older, well-publicized men who had begun to work with the ghetto. Neither thought highly of them. Beard told of one encounter with an important New York banker whose membership in a white-black coalition had been prominently advertised. Beard made a pitch to the banker to set up a section in his bank that would process small-loan applications from minority enterprises. "There's no progress going on in the city," he told the man. "Your bank could make a big difference."

"You really get lost if you get too much on the side of the blacks and Puerto Ricans," the banker replied.

"I've got good contacts with them," Beard argued.

"Yeah, but just remember where the power is," the banker said.

Beard remembered. The bank officer's refusal fresh in his ears, he went downstairs and sought out some younger bankers. They went to the ghetto, examined the loan applications, found them sound and put them through. To this day, their senior officer knows nothing of the loans.

"I want to charge off in all directions," Beard said now. "I would rather do ten things on the knowledge that I'll do one badly than sit around and analyze and do one thing perfectly." He described some other innovations:

"Louder Than Words Notes:" Capital Formation would pay 6–8 percent interest to anyone who would lend money for investment in the ghetto. Beard hoped to attract smaller investors who did not have the significant amounts of capital required by a limited partnership, but wanted to participate anyway.

"Corporate spinoffs:" encouraging U.S. corporations to farm out the manufacture of products or parts to ghetto proprietors. (CAN A GHETTO SPINOFF BE A PLUS ON YOUR PROFIT SHEET? asked a tantalizing foundation booklet. "Fifteen years ago, Puerto Rico was an economic wasteland. Today, successful Puerto Rican partnerships with American mainland firms are spreading prosperity through the island while profiting investors beyond any early imagination. Is the next new frontier for business development Harlem, Hough, Watts, Bedford-Stuyvesant?")

"I'd like to see five one-million-dollar funds," Beard dreamed aloud, "you running one, Larry running another, Fred running a third . . ."

He was talking shorthand now, but he was communicating, for "Larry" and "Fred" and the others were all young, impatient men who liked big risks and "feel the way we do," as the broker put it, about rich white America's responsibility to poor black.

White paternalism? Sam Beard shrugged. "Our board is white and black. If a guy doesn't want to work with us, that's his business."

The broker bought lunch. They walked to the street. Beard said goodbye, quickly, with apologies; he was late for another appointment. "My mother complained that I haven't called my answering service for twenty-one days," he said, laughing, and ran off into the swirling Wall Street crowd.

Each time our politicians and our media discover a new kind of American— the Silent American, the Radical American, the Middle American, the Backlash American—it would

seem that America is populated exclusively by that group. Is
it even necessary to suggest that all of these elements exist at
all times?

Certainly, some elements of our society are widely separated from others. But have they really "polarized" in recent
years, as is so often suggested? Is it not more likely that these
groups, reacting to the strident advocacy that dominates our
times, are simply vocalizing sentiments long submerged?

Certainly, thousands of young people today find it difficult or impossible to communicate with parents. But this
is hardly the first time in history the phenomenon has been
noted. Certainly, the most significant element of the young
generation, its educated elite, is adapting to values that much
of America cannot abide. But neither truth is enough to support the cherished thesis that the generations have been
chopped apart.

"Everything we know from the large studies of contemporary attitudes by pollsters and social scientists . . . leads
to the conclusion that the values and beliefs of parents and
children in this country in 1970 are far more in harmony
than in conflict," Richard Harwood of the *Washington Post*
wrote in July of that year. "One of the fascinating aspects of
the Gallup opinion summaries each month is the similarity
in the viewpoints of old and young. The disparities that crop
up are often surprising in their thrust." Harwood cited a
Gallup summary for May of 1970 indicating that the greatest
approval for President Nixon's performance comes from
people under thirty, and suggesting that this group, contrary
to belief, is the most hawkish in the country.

"On virtually all questions of this kind," Harwood
noted, "there is simply no evidence of any yawning 'generational gap.' " He cited an American Council on Education
query of 169,000 college freshmen in the fall of 1969 bearing

on the same point. "What came out of the council's statistical tables is a portrait of rather cautious and 'square' young men and women—rather like their parents, one suspects. Only one in twenty describes himself as a leftist or a rightist; the rest are in the great middle spectrum that runs from 'liberal' to 'moderately conservative.' " Harwood concludes: "None of these findings conforms to the myths and stereotypes promoted by both Yippies and intolerant elders that we are raising up generations of sybaritic revolutionaries in this country."

But if there is no universally experienced generational gap, there *is* a generational tradition. It is a tradition of change, whose custodians are those most forceful members of each generation who establish its challenge. It is they who show us where we are heading and determine our debates. It is they who flavor the age.

Certainly, the proportions of political elements at any given moment is important—important enough to affect local and national elections whose winners then guide the nation. But while these winners may alter the speed of travel, they rarely, if ever, can change our course.

We cannot locate ourselves by measuring today's antagonisms as expressed in the distances separating men. We can do that only by sizing the ideas around which they are gathered. Only when these ideas are compared to ideas years ago, can we see the distance we have traveled along the geography of time.

Nowhere is this exercise more essential than in locating the American Dilemma.

All through the elections of 1969, political commentators would tell us that the "backlash tide was sweeping across the frowning face of middle America." When John Lindsay won reelection in New York, the *Washington Post* remarked:

"The astounding reversal . . . sent analysts scurrying to their typewriters to explain how the 'year of the middle American' had suddenly started to look like the apotheosis of the sane liberal."

And what had John Lindsay said?

The basic drive that sends a man and his family out of starvation in Mississippi or destitution in San Juan is the same drive that brought the immigrants out of Europe, your ancestors and mine—the drive that makes a better life. . . . That effort to find a job, a home, a school, a society that lets man stand on his own—is part of the human spirit.

One of the more unbelievable interpretations of recent years was that ascribing a "backlash" victory to Mayor Sam Yorty of Los Angeles in his 1969 election contest against a Negro, Thomas Bradley. Admittedly, Yorty won because of his appeal to anti-Negro fear and prejudice on the part of the whites. But Bradley received 47 percent of the vote in a city that was only 18 percent black.

A few of our better young commentators appreciated this phenomenon. But none remarked on the simplest, most obvious, most historic fact of all. A *Negro* had run for mayor. We *have* Negro mayors now in major American cities. Twenty years ago they didn't exist.

Certainly, the number of elected and appointed black officials in the U.S. is not in proportion to the numbers of blacks. Yet, there they are: Mayors Carl B. Stokes in Cleveland, Richard Hatcher in Gary, Kenneth Gibson in Newark; Walter Washington runs Washington, D.C., and Thurgood Marshall, who argued the case for Negro school children before the U.S. Supreme Court, now sits on that court.

Twenty years ago, all-white primaries kept the majority of blacks from voting in local southern elections that mattered most to them. Today, thanks to the Supreme Court, to

Federal law enforcement, and to courageous voter-registration drives, southern black voters number more than 3.1 million —a sixfold increase in a decade—and 385 southern black officials now sit in city council, state legislature, and other elective seats where black men had never sat before.

Today, the racists fight one another with an idiotic, repugnant frenzy. But the long-range index line of the black man has been rising steadily for twenty-five years, since that opening day in Jersey City in 1946 when young Jackie Robinson of the Montreal Royals, adrenalin racing, went four for five, stole second twice, induced two run-scoring balks, and changed baseball, an image, and history.

The catalogue of specific gains is long and impressive— more black voters, more black officials, more black university graduates, more blacks in better jobs, blacks on southern juries, helping to convict whites for crimes against blacks. But the catalogue of need is so appalling that even to dwell on what has been accomplished risks complacency and deception.

Yet this poses an American dilemma all its own. Not to nourish on actual progress would be as wrong as to feast on the statistical tables of tokenism. Let us take it whole.

In 1870, eighty percent of all black Americans were illiterate. The figure today is 7 percent. But illiteracy among white Americans is less than 1 percent.

In 1930, black enrollment in colleges was 27,000. As of February, 1969, it was 275,000—a 1,000 percent increase in thirty-nine years. But the black college population is only 4 percent of the American college population of more than 6.5 million, whereas blacks constitute 10 percent of the American population.

In 1950, there were more states in which segregation in the public schools was mandatory than there were states in which school segregation was prohibited. Even in 1963, only one percent of black students were attending integrated southern schools. By 1969, of 2.5 million black school children in the Deep South, 518,607—20.3 percent—were attending integrated schools. Sixteen years after the 1954 U.S. Supreme Court decision outlawing segregation, there is not one state in which integration in the public schools, colleges, and universities does not exist. Yet the "compliance" is token in many, grudging in most, and constructive in few.

From 1962 to 1967, according to the *Monthly Labor Review* analysis made in 1969, Negro employment increased by 1 million, a gain of 14.4 percent; yet, in 1967, nearly half the employed Negroes were in unskilled, service, or farm jobs, while only a fifth of white workers held these types of jobs.

Negro unemployment dropped from 10.9 percent in 1962 to 7.4 percent in 1967; yet the 1967 rate was still about double the white rate. And the critically important teenage unemployment figure—between 25 and 30 percent—did not change at all.

About two-thirds of the net increase in employment for all Negro workers from 1962 to 1967 was in professional and technical, managerial, clerical, and sales occupations; yet in 1967, Negroes still represented only about 5.4 percent of all white-collar workers.

The number of Negro blue-collar craftsmen and operatives increased about 35 percent between 1962 and 1967. The bulk of this employment gain occurred in the operative group, however, where Negroes had already been employed in large numbers

In 1960, the median family income for blacks was $3,794, for whites, $6,857. By 1968, black median family income had risen to $5,359, but white median family income had risen to

$8,936. The 45 percent gap existing in 1960 had shrunk to only 40 percent in eight years.

In 1940, twenty-six American Federation of Labor unions constitutionally prohibited blacks from membership. Not one does today. Yet the legal fiction of employment equality is far from practical fact for blacks.

In 1968, the Department of Justice initiated twenty-five cases under the equal employment section of the 1964 Civil Rights Act. Only ten cases had been filed in the four previous years. More than half the cases were instituted in the North and West. Authorities believe that the legal action achieved an impact far beyond its numbers. Many employers began to comply with the law without official inducement. The results are conceivably more apparent to one who returns to the United States several times each year than to one who is constantly there. From executive offices to airline counters, he notices black people where black people never were before —a welcome sight however he may remind himself that if ours was a truly just society, 10 percent of those faces would be black.

But while the progress of the black man measured in such classical ways is important to the long-range resolution of the American dilemma, what is *critical* is the development of the black man's sense of himself. Only when he *feels* equal will the American dilemma end.

And that is the point where we may be in sizably better shape than the headlines tell us we are.

In the last days of 1969, I met an oral surgeon from New York at a party in St. Moritz. He told me that as part of his personal commitment to the resolution of the dilemma, he toured the South each year in search of a qualified black intern. His task was compounded by the reluctance of tech- nically well-qualified black men to accept the responsibility

that would focus on them in a small practice. They preferred
the anonymity of a big hospital.

The surgeon sighed. "How long do you think it will
take?" he asked me.

"A generation," I replied at once.

He shook his head. "No. Much longer than that."

Only the next morning did I realize that we had not
meant the same thing by "it."

He had meant the restructuring of the black community.
I had meant the restructuring of the white mentality to
blacks.

Each of us was right. The black community must approach equality with the white before the white will accept
it. The racist may tell you he was right all along with his
formula of "separate but equal" facilities. His argument errs
twice. The facilities were separate, only; never were they
equal. And any imposed structure could never have worked;
it had to be the black man's desire.

Less than two years after Martin Luther King's death, a
reporter asked Jesse Jackson, the heir-apparent to King's
leadership in the civil rights movement, whether King's
stress on the moral rather than the tactical aspects of the
civil rights movement had been a mistake.

"No," Jackson replied. "I think that even as recently
as 1966, Dr. King was correctly analyzing his problem as
the need to change the psyche of the black man. You couldn't
impress black folks unless you impressed white folks first. Dr.
King had to make the movement as large as possible in white
eyes to get respect for blacks."

Then Jackson, whose Operation Breadbasket, headquar-
tered in Chicago, has produced 5,000 jobs and $40,000,000 in an-
nual salaries for U.S. blacks, told his interviewer, "I think that
we are inclined to lose perspective on how much things have

changed since 1955. There was no black consciousness then."

Now that Negroes have discovered the psychological compulsion to be black, many abandon entirely the idea of integration, causing those blacks and whites who worked for integration to feel that years of their lives have been wasted. That is a superb example of swinging between extremes. A more fit approach is to recognize that a black man dignified by self-respect and suffused with self-assurance, an educated man with an awareness of others and no need to act out his aggressions, would be a much more attractive—*and* willing— candidate for integration.

The distance from now until then seems infinite. The journey is immensely complicated by a black revolutionary component that literally frightens whites, and by a pervasive naïveté among blacks about how white men make their living. Many conclude that whiteness automatically compels success; they have almost no idea of the effort and in-fighting that characterize the white man's career, and they do not seem conscious of the many whites who fail.

But because these attitudes exist, it does not mean they cannot be changed. If the conditions that created the attitudes would change, so might the attitudes themselves. That is where whites come in.

For the black man to achieve equality, or even a tolerable semblance, requires the help of the whites. The classical answer to that has been "never." "Never" will whites help blacks. That is a fact of life; it is simply the way things are.

It is precisely here that the vogue of despair is most dangerous. Using a convenient example from the morning newspaper, it confirms what it seeks to prove.

History suggests a better answer: We should be stirred by our victories and shocked by the needs.

Whatever man is basically by nature, he becomes something else by demand. Necessity first alerts him, then compels him to act—if only to save himself. Necessity exists today.

But so does a discredited quality called decency. Decency means that quantities of men, exposed to facts, will react in honorable ways. Tolerance was decent twenty years ago; acceptance is decent today.

Today, the new middle class—the skilled laborer making $10,000 a year, with money in the bank, in pension plans, in a home—fights the minority worker who competes for jobs. But the minority worker has the active sympathy now of many upper-middle-class whites.

When Senator Abraham Ribicoff of Connecticut returned home to campaign in 1968 following the finest hour of his life—his defiance of Chicago's Mayor Richard Daley at the Democratic convention—union workers cursed him. But residents of Litchfield county, rich and Republican, gave him standing ovations. So Ribicoff forsook traditionally Democratic labor groups and worked instead for the liberal Republican vote. He won reelection.

Elements of the American power Establishment are now in dialogue with blacks about how to make one society of two. Some of this is sheer public relations and riddled with insincerity, but much of it is substantial and helped by insights that simply did not exist within the Establishment twenty years ago. The Establishment man would tell you that welfare was a sop for people who really didn't wish to work. Today, even the most liberal Democrat must cheer a Republican who says, "Minorities really don't want prepared handouts, anyway. They want a chance at the starting line." That is a basis for dialogue between white and black— particularly when the speaker is Robert Finch, Richard Nixon's former Secretary of Health, Education, and Welfare, now a key White House aide.

"My public speech is not that way, because it's clear that you've got to keep the pressure on," Lew Douglass admitted one day. "To say we're making progress makes it sound almost like I'm a gradualist. But I think the fact is that we have a healthier society, even if no more than because we have a more honest dialogue going on, and a lot of people are thinking about the problems. I think that we're at a healthier position today than we were ten years ago, and then we were at a healthier position than we were twenty years ago. But we know that as a matter of strategy, we can't announce that we're satisfied."

The U.S. Government must help. So must the American Establishment. But something has happened within the last several years that is historically more vital to the resolution of the American Dilemma than the action of either. Ultimately, it will not be decency or even necessity that chiefly reduces racial tension in America to bearable levels. It will be the black man's belief in himself.

What America is attempting today has never before been accomplished. There is not one multiracial country in the world in which black and white live equally. In Brazil, they live harmoniously, but equality is a fiction; as in the U.S., color and poverty are soulmates.

It is right that America should try first. No white American can ever entirely comprehend the black American's psychological dilemma. But few people are as well equipped as white Americans to comprehend the need for acceptance. It is more than likely a need that they themselves have known. As immigrants, or sons of immigrants, or sons of sons of immigrants, they, too, have experienced the crisis of identity and the craving for acceptance whose unwilling inheritors today are black.

Some 40 million Americans of European descent consider themselves members of America's ethnic minority. There is evidence to suggest that the black man's search for identity has stimulated in them a new ethnic awareness. Rather than play the game according to Establishment rules—the first of which is to blend into the grain as expeditiously as possible—members of ethnic elements are coming to value their difference.

While most political assumptions in recent years have partnered ethnics and backlash, new findings do not support that relationship. The Louis Harris organization, in fact, has established the reverse, that native Anglo-Saxon Protestants are more inclined to be hostile to blacks than Irish, Italian, or Polish Americans. Half the Anglo-Saxon Americans polled thought efforts at equality too rapid. Ethnic groups were anywhere from eight to thirteen percentage points lower. One likely explanation for the result was that the ethnic groups could sympathize with the blacks' aspirations.

Perhaps the ethnic group whose rejection by the majority comes closest in degree to the blacks is the American Jew. In terms of background, motivation, and education, there is, of course, no parallel between blacks and Jews. But in terms of what pride can do for a minority, and of what pride, in turn, does to others' views of them, there is both a parallel and a lesson.

Each has known rejection. Each has found opportunity denied and self-respect decimated by a hostile world. Each requires a change in his image of himself before he can change the prevailing mentality. The black today is learning to accept and respect his uniqueness. It is only in the last twenty years that many U.S. Jews have learned to respect theirs.

A personal story will help me make my point.

When my mother was a seven-year-old girl in a Ukranian

village, townspeople set fire to her home. Not long thereafter, her two oldest brothers and a sister departed for America, where the streets were paved with gold. Her parents and five younger children soon followed. They arrived July 4, 1910.

When my mother was twenty-three, she married a thirty-seven-year-old Lithuanian immigrant, and like many of their kind, they worked hard at being Americans. My father, whose father and fathers before him were Orthodox rabbis, would not go to temple, and neither parent would teach me Yiddish.

I did not realize when I was eleven that I was a ghettoized Jew. Jews of that generation hid the fact of prejudice from children, just as blacks of the same generation would not say "Negro" when their youngsters were present. From the time I became thirteen, I learned very fast indeed. World War II erupted; my parents sent me to an Episcopal military academy; from the point of view of teaching me that I was different, it was a most effective school.

One day shortly before I left for the school I received a visit from a man whose son was about to start his third year there. He told me that I must be especially good so that I would make it that much easier for the next Jewish boy who went.

The forms of anti-Semitism are an old story, and I will not dwell on them here. Suffice it to say that every brutality and species of bigotry of which young Gentiles—and some of their teachers—were capable was visited upon me. The shock of my difference was so profound that by my last year in school I carried traces of anti-Semitism myself. If younger Jews received too many demerits, it was I who disciplined them.

I fought back, against the bigots, against myself. In this, I had the help of one professor, and several fellow cadets, not all of them close friends, yet each one precociously sensitive to the battle I was going through.

At the last parade, we seniors, Jews and Gentiles four years together, burned our gloves and, as tradition required, cried.

I left the school with a typically schizophrenic fighting Jewish hangup.

That summer, 1945, I enrolled at Northwestern and pledged a Jewish fraternity. The first lesson I learned was that no more than three Jews at a time were to congregate on campus together. Evenings, we would go to taverns to drink beer and listen to the Betas and Sigma Nu's sing their songs, but we would never sing ours. On V-J night, that folly reached its peak; we took the elevated train from Evanston to the Loop, and on the train we sang. But the word was passed and when the moment in the song came to sing the fraternity's name, we sang Beta Theta Pi instead, a perfect substitute in rhythm and rhyme for the one we were ashamed, before strangers, to sing.

That fall, upset by these attitudes, I transferred to UCLA. I spoke to the Dean of Men, and asked him to recommend a Jewish fraternity whose members were proud to be Jews.

Some were. Some were not. The same self-consciousness existed there, the same self-deprecation and bewilderment, the same ambivalent desire to pass, to assimilate, to be like the others. Most of the Jews at UCLA stood in the shade in front of the library; we stood in the sun with the Gentiles on the steps of Royce Hall.

What changes the years have produced!

One November morning in 1964, I noticed Bill Arthur, who was then *Look's* managing editor, standing mournfully in the frame of his office door. By then, Dan Mich, the editor, was dying, and Bill was already in charge. "You look depressed," I said. "What's the matter?"

"I need a coverline for the Christmas issue," Bill said.

"You want a coverline? I'll give you a coverline," I said.

"Will you?" he said.

I had thought he was joking. I *had* been joking. But now I returned to my office and closed the door. Twenty minutes later we closed his office door. I read the coverline.

"The Jew and Christmas?" Bill said. "What's that about?"

This is how the answer appeared in *Look.*

For U.S. Jews, the massively ironic question of Christmas remains the deeply personal one of how they feel about being Jews. Every December, millions of them—even some of the Orthodox—are tugged two ways. As Americans, they yearn to join their Christian brothers in outpourings of goodwill and grog. As Jews, admit it or not, they experience the annual shock of recognition that they are in alien territory. The taut wire between doubt and desire frequently snaps. Rabbis lecture congregants, children nag parents, husbands battle wives. . . . To be against Santa Claus seems almost un-American, and to U.S. Jews, that is no joke. . . .

Reporting the story was one of the most rewarding experiences of my life. That evening I was on an airplane for Los Angeles, for a reunion with UCLA classmates I hadn't seen in years. For the next several weeks I covered the United States, visiting old haunts and friends, rabbis, sociologists—anyone who could help me in my quest. I had not known what I would find when I started, but when I had finished, the findings were unmistakable.

Employment, housing and social restrictions had been

slowly lifting, and the U.S. Jew was experiencing what a student of the subject described as "an unprecedented feeling of acceptance, legitimacy and justification. There is a growing sense that a place is being made for him in the structure of the democratic process. The change in the status of the Jew is nowhere more clearly symbolized than in the emerging Jewish attitude towards Christmas."

. . . Sure of themselves as their parents never were [I wrote later], the Jews of the new generation now tend to reject Christmas celebrations in Jewish homes as unseemly. . . . Among organized Jewry, at least, it is the overwhelming impression of their leaders that the Christmas paradox is being resolved. . . .

The second-generation American Jew fled his father's ghetto, changed his name, refused to teach his children Yiddish. In extreme cases, Jews who resented being born to a life of difference turned on those whose fate they shared. More frequently, many Jews were simply afraid to be themselves. . . .

But today the talk is no longer of self-hatred but of a sociological principle known as Hansen's Law: What the son wishes to forget, the grandson wishes to remember. This third-generation Jew neither sounds nor feels inferior. He looks American, nourishes on security and has the strength to ask, "Who am I?" Inevitably the quest for identity leads back to his roots.

Conversations with Jews across the U.S. revealed a feeling of pride almost unknown twenty years before. Jewish leaders all had pet stories of young groups of Jews openly identifying as such—wearing sweatshirts with Hebrew lettering, camping out in a *sukkah,* inviting Gentile friends to assist with artwork for rallies of Jewish youth. Almost invariably, the tale would end with the remark, "I never would have done that." Rabbi Henry Skirball, associate director of youth affairs for the Union of American Hebrew Congregations explained: "You don't see as much self-hatred now as you did in our generation. We're a whole generation removed from the Eastern European Jew who was proving his Americanism. We're at the crest of an organizational surge. Our kids don't feel out of it. They can affiliate. They don't feel square. Between 1925 and 1930, it was something if 50 percent of the college kids would put down 'Jewish' if they were asked to state their religious affiliation. Today, they all do."

There was a report from the Hillel Foundation: "Thirty or forty years ago, young Jews were largely in flight. The campus populations in those days was overwhelmingly non-Jewish. . . . The lines of demarcation between Jews and Christians were sharply defined. In this setting, being Jewish meant being strange. It meant the experience of Judaism as a handicap in one's effort to gain an American identity . . . Today's students are no longer in flight . . . The phrase 'hemorrhage of Jewish loyalty' among college students is a matter of past history." The provost of Hebrew Union College, Dr. Samuel Sandmel, told me, "In the 1960s, being Jewish is in no way a barrier. Their non-Jewish friends now find Jews exotic."

So many factors had caused the change—the martyrdom of the Jews at the hands of Hitler; the story of bravery being written in Israel; novels about Jews by Jews, some romanticizing them excessively, most dealing with them sensitively. Within the theological world, so great was the impact of Jewish thinkers like Martin Buber on Protestants and Catholics that, as Rabbi Robert Katz of Cincinnati put it, "The feedback from the non-Jewish world is such as to compel the Jew to rediscover what he has tried to forget."

It was this rediscovery that was leading American Jews to reject the assimilationist ways of their parents. A young Jewish matron who had grown up in a Gentile suburb near New York recalled listening to Christmas carols with clammy hands when she was small. "I'd never have a tree now," she told me. An Illinois man declared, "Putting a tree in my house would be like changing my name from Jack Golfarb to Jordan Gray." Said the rabbi at a neighboring synagogue: "After you get somewhere, the tree gets smaller. It's no longer decorous to 'goy it up.' Changing names and noses and having trees were inadequate ways of handling the problem. The kids will have nothing to do with it." A San Francisco manufacturer recalled preparing for a Christmas party, a traditional dinner for members of the city's Jewish community. Because his wife was late, the man stepped outside to wait. "There I was in my well-pressed tuxedo, and out came this Gentile from next door in his well-pressed tuxedo. I almost fainted. I asked myself, 'What am I doing here?' "

No episode remains more vividly in my mind than one in the home of a very old friend who for years had observed the holiday. "By my celebrating Christmas I get the feeling that I am for a moment a part of white Protestant America," he admitted. "For a day I say to myself, 'This is what the world is celebrating;' I don't enjoy being different." Suddenly, he turned to his teenage daughter. "Supposing I said 'I've decided that we've been avoiding the reality of who we are and what we are, and so we're not going to celebrate Christmas any more.' What would you say?"

"Nothing would please me more," she replied at once. Her father seemed stunned. She went on, "I want to be taken for what I am. I'm proud to be a Jew. When I move out I will not celebrate Christmas. I feel like a hypocrite."

Rabbis and Jewish educators were keenly feeling the new challenge of unself-conscious Jewish youngsters. Judaism, they were finding, had to be made relevant in ways it had not been before, for while the young may not have an identity problem, they might reject Judaism for other reasons.

What is historic, however, is that the young Jew of today

is psychologically free to choose on the high ground of commitment. He can be different, or not different, as he desires. The same force that frees him to forget a Christmas tree also frees him to seek a firm foundation for his faith.

The day Lew Douglass described his attempts to disperse black students at the Brooklyn College cafeteria, my mind flew back to the steps of UCLA's Royce Hall. I blurted, "Man, you don't know! You're telling me the story of my life."

Once, Lew was remembering: "Ten years ago, if you had a party and you were young and sophisticated, what made your party fashionable was to have white people come."

I laughed. "What made my party fashionable was to have a black guy."

"Yes, I remember all the jokes about Negroes for hire. And it worked on our side, too. You'd go through all kinds of changes to make sure that you had some white liberals at the party. I can remember planning a party with my wife and figuring, 'How many white people do we have here?' We would even say, because Negro parties run late—as a matter of habit they start at 11 and go 'til about 3, and white parties start at 8 and run to about 1—we would always say, 'Well, the white people will leave about 12:30 or 1 o'clock, and then the real party will start.' I don't think people really care anymore. But the funny thing about it is, there are more real friendships developing today, where people are just becoming friends."

"You know what I think?" I said. "We really had to go through this experience to a time where we could look back and laugh at ourselves and say, 'Hey, I was inviting you to my party to be fashionable, and you were inviting me to your party to be fashionable. But we never would have said it at the time."

Today, with racial animosity at fever pitch, it is hard to believe that a white-black détente could arrive.

It is harder still when our media stimulate us to fix our eye on the dot of today rather than cast it across the round curve of time.

But once we do cast, we catch a different sense of our times.

In Western societies, each conservative regime comes to power at a time when society needs to digest and consolidate what the liberals have done to change it. The conservatives adapt themselves to the liberal reforms of their predecessors. The cycle is one of reform, consolidation, reform, consolidation, not reform, reaction, reform, reaction. What we see is a movement ever left, prodded by radicals, consolidated by liberals, institutionalized by conservatives.

That $10,000-a-year auto worker may not wish to recall it, but it was less than forty years ago that Walter Reuther and his union organizers fought violent battles with company police at the plant where he now works. The battles angered and upset and catalyzed many Americans of the silent majority then, just as do radical efforts today. But thanks to such battles, American management now understands that good wages mean prosperity for all. What sensible observer of forty years ago would have forecast the amicability—indeed, the dangerous amicability—that permeates U.S. labor-management relations today?

Change occurs across the board. To compare the Republican party platform of 1928 with the party's platform of 1968 is to learn a startling lesson in the metamorphosis of contemporary thought.

1928: "We affirm our belief in the protective tariff as a fundamental and essential principle of the economic life of this nation . . . It has stimulated the development of our natural resources, provided fuller employment at higher wages through the promotion of industrial activity, assured thereby the continuance of the farmer's major mark and further raised the standards of living and general comfort of our people. The great expansion in the wealth of our nation during the past fifty years, and particularly in the last decade, could not have been accomplished without a protective tariff system designed to promote the vital interests of all classes."

1968: "It remains the policy of the Republican party to work toward freer trade among all nations of the free world . . . A sudden influx of imports can endanger many industries.. These problems, differing in each industry, must be considered case by case. Our guideline will be fairness for both producers and workers, without foreclosing imports."

Foreign policy, 1928: "The Republican Party maintains the traditional American policy of non-interference in the political affairs of other nations. The government has definitely refused membership in the League of Nations and to assume any obligations under the covernant of the League.

"On this we stand. . . ."

Foreign policy, 1968: "Our best hope for enduring peace lies in comprehensive international cooperation. We will consult with nations that share our purposes. We will press for their greater participation in man's common concerns and encourage regional approaches to defense, economic development and peaceful adjustment of disputes.

"We will seek to develop law among nations and strengthen agencies to effectuate that law and cooperatively solve common problems. We will assist the United Nations to become the keystone of such agencies . . ."

Richard Nixon, when he took office, said he would not undo the past. He couldn't if he tried. He may temporarily revert to fiscal orthodoxy to curb inflation, but he subsequently turns to Keynesian deficit finance to overcome the economic slump that ensues. His political existence requires him to convince the American worker, the minority, and even the middle class that he will not repeal the social gains of the New Deal, the Fair Deal, or the Great Society. To keep his pledge, he must embrace a moderately liberal program of reform built on the same foundation. Some characteristics of this reform show significant historic change.

In August, 1969, President Nixon offered a welfare program guaranteeing a family of four then on welfare, with no outside income, a federal payment of $1,600 a year, which the states could supplement if they wished. Outside earnings were to be encouraged, not discouraged. The new worker could keep the first $60 a month in outside earnings with no reduction in his benefits, and 50 cents of each dollar thereafter.

The President's welfare concepts were far more than a program. They were an admission that poverty is an expression of society's failure—and that society must assume responsibility for its faults. Irrespective of the program's momentary political fate, the existence of the *concepts* measures the distance thought has traveled from the time, not too long ago, when the idea that poverty was an expression of indolence was part of the conservative creed.

Of all the conflicting signals being broadcast today, here perhaps, is the strongest. It not only indicates our increasing willingness to meet problems in ways heretofore unacceptable, it locates us in the geography of time.

Relative positions have not changed. *What has changed is the location of the center.*

What force moved the center? What force moved the

country? Conceivably it was decency. Undoubtedly, it was necessity. Probably, it was a measure of each.

Whether decency impels us, or necessity compels us, we know we must resolve our dilemma. There are many avenues to the solution. It is not a question of either/or—either separation or integration. Each has a function and time. The black man may very well need to "go through the black bag," as Lew Douglass put it, before he can stand proud. For the white man, the answer is much simpler: He must invest in better neighbors. A man whose needs are fulfilled will make a better neighbor than a man whose needs are not. This investment we are now prepared to make.

But the money required to resolve the American Dilemma is invested in the American Obsession—to save the world for Democracy—at a ratio of 10 to 1.

It is time now to look at the American Obsession.

Since, 1946, when Winston Churchill announced in Fulton, Missouri, that an Iron Curtain had descended on Eastern Europe, our fate, our fortune, and ultimately the quality of our lives have turned on Russian designs.

So let us begin in that strange place. Let us then move westward through Eastern Europe and back to the United States.

CHAPTER FIVE

THE OTHER SIDE OF
THE CURTAIN

To even the practiced eye, the surface of Moscow yielded pleasant and reassuring glimpses in the summer of 1969. Gardner "Mike" Cowles, *Look's* founder and editorial chairman, arrived there on his sixth trip since 1935. Two had been notable. In 1942, in the company of Wendell Willkie, Mike Cowles had lived for several days in the Kremlin as the guest of Josef Stalin; one night Stalin had led them to the parapets of the Kremlin to watch the flash of German artillery. In 1962, Mike Cowles had entered the Kremlin again for a three-and-one-half-hour visit with Nikita Khrushchev; his exclusive interview had made headlines. Now he was back in Moscow, on vacation with his wife, Jan, and daughter, Virginia. But he had requested an interview with the present Soviet premier, Alexei Kosygin. I joined him in Moscow to help write the story, should the request be granted.

As we waited, we toured the city. Mike Cowles was impressed. The people, he said, appeared better dressed, groomed, and fed than he had ever remembered. One evening Jerry Shechter, *Time's* affable Moscow correspondent, invited us to his apartment on the outskirts of the city for dinner. Mike Cowles stood on Jerry's lofty terrace, gazed out over the cluster of high-rise buildings, and shook his head, remembering; those artillery flashes could have come from just about here. A few nights later, we watched a floor show at the newest Intourist supper club: a prancing chorus line of leggy girls, singers, acrobats, jugglers, comedians; and that Big Band sound, first the reeds, then the brass, standing—in blazers—to swing a chorus. "That show," said Mike, "might have been put on twenty years ago at the Chez Paree in Chicago."

One afternoon we drove to the Rossiya Hotel, the modern colossus next to Red Square, rode an elevator to the seventh floor, and walked a quarter mile of corridors, past doors shielding tiny but comfortable rooms, to a glassed-in buffet overlooking the Kremlin. It took half an hour to get two beers; I had to wait in line while the single woman attendant first served orders of caviar and halves of broiled chicken to the guests ahead of me. Evenings, there was ballet or the circus, and, if one thought ahead sufficiently to make reservations, good Georgian or Uzbekistan food. If not, there was always the special room for tourists at the Hotel Metropole, where one ate superb blinis and caviar while a chorus sang from the balcony overhead. Indeed, the tourist passing in and out of Moscow during the summer of 1969 might return home wondering what all the headlines were about.

They were ominous headlines, and they were true. It took only a week of probing in the conspiratorial, sinister layers beneath the tourist surface to convince us. After golden years of relative openness, extending through the era of Nikita Khrushchev and even into the early Brezhnev-Kosygin rule—years of improved contacts with the West, of economic experiment at home, of increasingly rational and civilized conduct—Russia, as it had so many times during its malevolent past, had once more turned its dark side to the world.

Since the invasion of Czechoslovakia, the Voice of America had been jammed. Foreigners residing in Moscow had been cut off from contact with all but a few official Russians. Unabashed Stalinists had once again moved into the key editorial slots. Soviet newspapers excoriated intellectuals in Communist countries who had the temerity to think for themselves, demanded they close their minds to information from the West, and promised decisive action against those who "confused" the right of socialist criticism with the "unrestrained dissemination of antisocialist ideas." Already, the neo-Stalinists had suppressed numerous films, withdrawn plays, deleted works of poetry. Under their direction, writers with worldwide reputations had faded from print. Russians rarely saw the works of Yevgheny Yevtushenko, Andrei Voznesensky, Bella Akhmadulina, three poets who had been required reading for those who follow the evolution of Russian intellectual thought. The greatest loss was Alexander Solzhenitsyn, whose action novel *One Day in the Life of Ivan Denisovich* had rendered the horrors of life under Stalin for the millions he imprisoned and killed. Neither *First Circle* nor *Cancer Ward,* the novelist's later works, had been published in the Soviet Union. Solzhenitsyn was now in seclusion.

Sinyavsky, Daniel, Ginzburg, Bukovsky, and Litvinov— intellectuals who had protested—had all been tried and sentenced. The scientist, Medvedev, was to be railroaded to a mental institution, to be saved later from a lifetime of confinement only by the heroic protests of Solzhenitsyn and Andrei Sakharov, a courageous Russian physicist. Other, less important trials had received no publicity at all. For the active protesters, punishment meant exile, or commitment to an asylum, or imprisonment at hard labor. Milder forms of dissent, such as the signing of petitions against the country's intrusion in Czechoslovakia, were punished by dismissal from jobs, interruption of careers, loss of scarce apartments, or banishment from the cities. There seemed no likelihood that the mass killings of Stalinist days would be repeated, but this was small consolation to those whose lives were being ruined.

Russia's leaders were acting with the characteristics of men who had botched their jobs, and were striving feverishly to protect them.

They had provoked a war in the Middle East that could have been avoided, and given indications that they were not in control of events there, even though the war could not have been undertaken without their help.

They had made an egregious blunder in Czechoslovakia. The piousness with which they had heretofore proclaimed the principle of noninterference in the affairs of other countries had been rendered useless; in its place was the maddening Brezhnev doctrine: A Communist country may choose freely, so long as it chooses Russia's brand of communism; it may seek its own solutions, unless these solutions conflict with the interests of other Communist countries within the Russian orbit. The Soviet Union will decide when such interests are in conflict.

Moreover, the Russian leaders had worked themselves into an open clash with Red China. To those peoples who had worried and sacrificed against the threat of Red aggression, the prospect of war between these two Communist giants might almost have seemed delicious—until they thought of the inhuman consequences of a nuclear war, and the possibility that such a war would ultimately involve all.

Seven years earlier, Mike Cowles had been summoned to the Kremlin on the last day of his visit to see Nikita Khrushchev. On the last day of this visit, I received a call from my Russian contact: "Mr. Cowles will not see Premier Kosygin on this trip," he said. "You will understand why when you see the headlines tomorrow." The next day, Washington announced President Nixon's forthcoming visit to Rumania.

Mike Cowles and I left the Soviet Union more depressed than on any previous trip.

It would be fair, logical, and likely for any Westerner confronted with such evidence to conclude that the Soviet people would be frightened, dismayed, resentful, disillusioned, and ready to rise in revolt. It would be fair, logical, and likely, but in all probability, it would be wrong.

It would be substituting wish for reality—the unconscious, pervasive wish to see an opposing idea proved wrong. It would assume that others react to events of which they are a part as we would react to them if we were a part. Some do. The overwhelming majority do not.

The current protests by intellectuals against suppression of liberty are heroic, poignant, and important components of contemporary Russian reality. But to be accurately gauged they must be placed in the context of an accepting, believing society, addicted by centuries of rule and religious habit to authoritarian structures—of which the Communist totalitarian system is the latest variant. The average Russian is as likely to sympathize with his country's protesting intellectuals as a resident of Orange County, California, will sympathize with the Free Speech Movement at Berkeley.

The headlines on "neo-Stalinism" obscure a crushing fact —that to the Russian masses, the protest is of little consequence. They would not participate in it if they could. They do not particularly concern themselves with its outcome. As Larissa Daniel, the wife of writer Yuri Daniel, was sentenced to four years in exile for her protests, she "drew attention," according to a news report, "to what most dissidents consider an enemy even greater than the regime. That is the pervasive conformity of all but a fraction of the nation of 236 million people."

It has been one of the assumptions by which our lives have been structured that the average Russian is a captive who would gladly overthrow his system in favor of a more democratic one. The assumption is wrong—and dangerous. As Averell Harriman has written: "Misunderstandings . . . feed on die-hard myths, such as the one so many Americans cling to—that the Soviet people are ready to rise up and overthrow their Communist leaders if the West would give them enough encouragement."

Why do such "die-hard myths" prevail? Chiefly, I think, because we reject reality in favor of what we would *like* to believe and, by applying our own values to others' conditions, "justify" our logic. But to project the values of a Western democrat onto Soviet people today is a futile gesture; to assume they will react in a certain way to circumstances because that is the way you would react is to fall headlong into the worst of logical traps.

I've suggested that real dialogue occurs not when you look at reality through the eyes of someone with whose way of looking at the world you can identify, but when you look at it through the eyes of someone with whose way of looking at the world you can't. Only when you step out of your own traces and into those of another human being can you perceive outside your own set of givens. Only then does dialogue —and communication—occur.

Nowhere is a leap into the other's skin more necessary than in the effort to understand Russians. For the average Russian may not be what the Communists set out to make him, but he is very different from you and me. He has blended the demands of ego and the discipline of sacrifice so that group instincts prevail over self. He wants a lot, but not an awful lot. He worships science and belittles faith, but he is nothing if not a believer. Independent thought makes him uncomfortable. He may bellow his disagreement on a local matter, but when it's Russia against the world, he naïvely, uncritically— and patriotically—follows the leader. Sophisticated Russians reacted with horror and despair to Russia's 1968 invasion of Czechoslovakia. But the man in the street accepted the official version of events and castigated the Czechs, who had been liberated from the Nazis by Russian troops, for their lack of "gratitude." Age has not mellowed the Soviet sense of righteousness; there is no more illuminating, or infuriating, experience than to suggest that Western actions since 1945 have been a response to hostile Communist thrusts—only to have Russians laugh in your face. They cannot believe that Stalin, the murderer they denounced at home, might also have committed crimes abroad. They genuinely fear dictatorship, but they retain a child's faith in their dictators. Dissent flourishes—about means, not ends. They still believe in the ultimate triumph of communism over capitalism, but not in a triumph of violence. Their wartime suffering remains vivid; their horror of nuclear war, pervasive. A good Marxist does not export revolution, they will tell you. Vindication, not conquest, is their aim, and through evolution, they say, they will have it.

We have a vision of a sour country of no smiles and grudging consent and a helplessness in face of the inevitable. And I have known many critics, malcontents and rebels. But it is time we recognize that a lot of Russians believe in what they're doing. They feel protected. They are not worried about going hungry or being deserted or having some financial calamity befall them. Raised in a controlled environment, they are without objective measure, but by their own meager reckoning of what constitutes freedom, many of them now feel free.

"What exists in Russia today," George Kennan observed in *Foreign Affairs* on the fiftieth anniversary of the Revolution of 1917, "is, in so far as any political regime can form the character of a human community, the product of its endeavor. Russian society today is something that draws heavily on historical experience and national tradition, but it also reflects, in features that are probably now ineradicable, the influence of the ideologically impassioned political will to which it has been subjected over five decades. It is in reality a civilization rather than just a national society that has been thus created—a unique civilization, not quite like anything else in the world, imperfect like every other, in many ways unsatisfying to those that bear it, but also embracing many aspects in which they take pride and satisfaction, and even some that they cherish. Its salient features have already achieved in many respects that sanction which only time and long acceptance can bestow on human institutions."

Go to a jammed celebration of V-E day at a Moscow stadium. The reenactment of victory over the Germans at a cost of 20 million Russian lives evokes roaring cheers. These are not party hacks clacking; they are Russians celebrating salvation.

Or walk from the National Hotel in Moscow. Outside stand two actors, dressed in shabby overalls, waiting to appear in a scene of a motion picture. Instinctively, my colleague Paul Fusco raises his camera. Out of a corner of my eye, I note a handsome young man walking toward us. My gaze rivets on him. He is just passing when I can almost literally see the thought hit him. He stops, wheels, and throws his briefcase in front of Paul's lens. He pushes Paul and shouts at him. To a gathering crowd he storms at the foreigner taking photographs that emphasize the poorer aspects of Russian society. It is five minutes before he can be persuaded to leave Paul alone. He departs, muttering and unconvinced.

Or sit among a full house of Soviets laughing at a movie. It's their adventure they're thrilling to, filtered through a special vision. It's propaganda, but *they* like it. They can't be told enough that they are moral, heroic, daring, just. The movie, *The Avengers,* depicts four children, fourteen, perhaps, who take on gangs of bad men during the postrevolutionary civil war. The style is Russian Western—fights and chases, a drunken barroom scene, a dance, a brawl. The young avengers kill everyone—three men with one bullet—and we cut to headquarters of the Red Army, where standing in overcoats twice their size, they receive the accolade of a Russian Red general whose benevolence has earlier been established.

How the audience laughs and claps, and as the four young avengers ride off into the sunset and the houselights rise, these Russians exude the feeling (stretching, chuckling, grinning) of an audience that has been entertained.

Arguments about where Russia might have been without the revolution do not impress her people. They say they would not have shared in the proceeds. That's what they have been told, and that's what they believe. I once met a Russian named Ivan Butrin who had been a World War II pilot. When he entered the Air Force, his mother, a peasant, took him to the depot. Very few pilots were returning at this time, so when she kissed him goodbye, she crossed him. "What on earth did you do that for?" he said.

"Well, I don't know," she answered. "I don't believe in God, but apparently people did in the generation before me, and maybe there's something in it, so I'm not going to take chances."

His mother, a janitress, had learned to read and write in 1937 at the age of forty-one. All her sons have college degrees. "If you want to raise the question of what the October revolution did to the Soviet Union, you can consider my family," Ivan said. "If it weren't for the revolution, I would be a shepherd."

Three generations of Russians have been taught to fear the gift of uniqueness within themselves. Until you understand this fear, you can neither understand them, nor how vastly they differ from us.

Let me relate three episodes that I believe will make the point.

The goal of education in the Soviet Union is to meet manpower needs and develop loyal, reliable citizens, to use the words of a Harvard University study. Our own goal is to develop a skeptical, intellectually curious, free-roving intelligence. The debate about which is better has a dry quality to it until you see the kids—as I did one summer afternoon.

We went to the opening ceremonies of a Pioneer camp near Bratsk, and I shall not forget a nine-year-old boy, bugle to his lips, hand on hip, blowing a staccato one-note in time to drums. Five hundred and forty kids marched in to the ceremony square and stood in the shade of lofty pines while the camp commander, the director of physical education, shouted commands, and the spokesmen for each unit (thirteen in all) reported his unit's strength and nature and then called for his unit to shout its motto ("Friendship, Courage, Valor, Honor." . . . "Always forward, not a step back." . . . "A hero will never die, he will carry the banner forward proudly." . . . "To struggle and seek, never to yield." . . . "Wherever the road is hardest, our detachment leads the way." . . . and, appropriately, "More do, less words.")

After the units had reported and the counselors had

been heard from ("Which other profession is required to start the hearts of young children flaming?"), the senior counselor of the camp requested permission to declare the camp open. The camp director stepped forward (print dress, red hair, ruby earrings, and 170 pounds on a short frame) and said, "The permission is granted." Then the director received the banner, which a color guard of ten-year-olds paraded about, and to the tune of the Internationale and an intolerably squeaky pulley the children raised the Soviet flag. The director wished the children good health, a good rest, and plenty of enterprise; the Komsomol leader of Bratsk, a shortsighted blond of twenty-five, wished them more health and endurance from their brother Komsomols, who hoped they would learn about their mothers and fathers who had built the Bratsk power station; and the Communist party leader, a tall, balding man of forty-five, told the children that he had been to Pioneer camp only once in his life—in June of 1941. "I wish that that month will never be repeated again." He added, "Great things are in store for you. Get prepared. It is never too early to start."

And then a young leader announced, "Young Leninists, be ready for the struggle of the cause of the Communist Party." And suddenly, the 540 children snapped their arms in front of their faces—an almost military salute—and shouted," *Vsegda gotovy.*" It means "Always ready," and it is the Pioneers' motto. And that is a moment for a lover of kids to be sad.

Soviet society seems so foreign to the nature of man. But the average Russian prefers it to a degree we would not imagine. It satisfies a singularly Russian taste for the assumption of responsibility by the state in the arena of public welfare—an urge that predates by far the Revolution of 1917. If to this trait is attached a sense of identity, patriotism, glamour, and an overwhelming stress on responsibility to the group, that little nine-year-old bugler doesn't have a chance. He will be content, but he will be dull. What he might have been he will never be.

Consider the responses of six young girls from a secondary school I met a few days after my visit to the Pioneer camp. I asked what concerned them most. They answered peace. I asked what was the most influential force in their lives, family or society. Three said family, two said society, and one refused to subdivide. I asked them what they would tell their children. They replied in an unusual and revealing form.

Parents should listen to the voices of their children. Children should be brought up with a desire to gain knowledge. Parents should teach honesty from the start. Parents should bring up their children like Spartans. Parents should be kind. Parents should instill a principled attitude in their children, and teach them to stand by their ideals.

And what, I asked, if these ideals were independently theirs?

"If these ideals act against the interests of society, the person should be reeducated," one of the girls replied. All the others agreed.

This same unrelenting emphasis on the group is even more pronounced among adults. I have observed the phenomenon many times, but never more forcefully than during one evening discussion at the home of a forty-one-year-old engineer named Yevgheny Vereshagen. Participants included his next-door neighbor, who, like Vereshagen, was temporarily without his wife; his brother, an excavator, much younger, very muscular, with a blazing smile heightened by skin deeply burnished from outdoor work; and the brother's girl friend, a soft, buxom, terribly pretty blond of twenty-five named Jana. It suddenly seemed a good time to talk about careers and marriage.

I asked if a conflict existed for women. We'd heard so many stories of newlyweds getting separated, the man to a job in Place A, the woman to a job in Place B. This might do wonders for careers, but it didn't seem a promising start to marriage. "How about it?" I asked Jana. "Are you concerned about femininity, about raising a family?"

She certainly was, Jana said, but she felt she could make career and marriage coincide.

"Does a woman really want to achieve like a man in this society?" I asked.

"Yes," Jana said. "I want to achieve. I feel in many ways that I'm equal to a man. I want to contribute."

"Well, let's make a stark situation," I said. "If you had to choose between a career and a family—you absolutely could not have both—which would you choose?"

"Family," Jana said.

I felt like kissing her.

But I don't think the other men did. For several minutes, they argued among themselves, all but ignoring me. Yes, they conceded, they wanted feminine women. But a woman had to make a contribution to society. And suddenly Vereshagen's neighbor had the floor. He'd been dropping little hints earlier that indicated a poor marriage. Now he talked of the hardship he and his wife had endured when they'd volunteered to help settle some lands in the Kazistan desert. He was in charge of construction for the settlement. Within months after their child was born, his wife was demanding that he have a nursery built, and she kept after him until he did. Then she returned to work.

"Does this arrangement give you the quality you want to marriage?"

"Well, if my wife didn't work, why, we'd have nothing to talk about in two or three years. Today, my wife understands the good half of my life, but imagine a different picture. I come back from work, my head is full of problems, and my wife says, 'Oh, gee, you should have seen the hat our neighbor had, and I certainly want to buy a hat like that.' I want tidy rooms and I want tidy kids and I want a house run efficiently but, my heavens, I want a wife who can talk to me about my problems."

Then Vereshagen said, "I want a well-laid table. If my wife works as much as I do I have to help her. I don't like that at all. If I have the opportunity to get service I'm going to do so. I think that's the answer. We've got to improve our services. I think we should have children's services included."

"What kind of children does that make?" I asked. "In its earliest years, particularly, the child needs mother love. Now what choice do you want *here,* where the child's welfare is involved?"

The opinions tumbled out.

"Bringing up the child in a collective helps to eliminate 'harmful individuality,' " the neighbor said.

"Man is a herd animal," Vereshagen said. "The elements of self-seeking and egoism are ingrained in the nature of the human being. The child who lives within the context of the family tends to pronounce 'this is mine' very very often. If it spends most of its time within the collective, however, the tendency is observed more rarely. This child comes to relate to the people around him; if he doesn't he becomes a bad friend, if he does he becomes a good friend. If he's within a collective he becomes not narrow, he becomes broader."

I understood the necessity of teaching a child his obligation to society, I said. But by such total emphasis, do you not lose something? The individual is never reinforced in his desire for individuality.

Vereshagen said, "Close contact with the collective tends to stimulate one's individuality."

"There's no contradiction," the neighbor said. "You have a great deal of happiness in your society. You obviously have values that you teach. We just think we teach them better. The normal tendency of a child in your society is to demonstrate his superiority over his peers. In our society this normal tendency is blunted by the obligation to raise others to your own level."

"Our social system is quite new," Vereshagen said. "Even if the individual doesn't display creative talent and individuality, he still retains the capacity for material well-being. The major trouble is that during the period of our history we haven't managed to eradicate the tendency for self-gratification, destructive egoism. We haven't completely managed to channel the individual's egoistic instincts into socially creative norms."

There is yet another reason why Russians react very differently to their reality than we, applying our logic, would imagine they do. I have touched on it already, but I think it bears repeating:

There is a mighty force in man that compels him to accept what he has and is, because to challenge that is to tear him loose from the moorings of his life.

Given the realities of life, Russians must seek fulfillment with the System. Whether some silent, interior struggle precedes their submission is possible, but unlikely.

Gennady Matushin is a tall, broad, blond, balding, pleasant, eager, impractical, well-meaning but inefficient, loyal, and zealous worker. He was born in Leningrad. His father died in 1942 of starvation during the siege of the city. That spring, Gennady, fourteen, took his mother in a truck with thirty-five other people over the river on the ice. But the ice was melting and the truck pushed the ice under water. They looked like they were riding on the water. Many other trucks stalled. Gennady's made it. He finished seven years of school in Moscow, all that were offered at the time. Then technical school, where he learned to design aircraft weaponry. Drafted in 1950. Discharged in 1953. Studied English four years at Foreign Language School in Leningrad. Back to Moscow and two years with a cultural exchange program. Hated it. Bailed out by friends to translation work in trade union movement. Then foreign service in India. Finally, Novosti Press Agency, Moscow, where part of his work is to read the Western press.

One day in Siberia, Gennady read a story to Paul Fusco and me about the strafing of a Soviet freighter in Haiphong harbor by two American aircraft. He was highly disturbed. He felt the action had been deliberate. He said the war in Vietnam was really a war against the Soviet Union. He had read that very argument in the U.S. press. It turned out that he had read David Lawrence, a conservative publisher and columnist.

We suggested that he shouldn't base his ideas of the U.S. on David Lawrence. He said that if Lawrence's view was not correct, he should not be permitted to publish it. In his country, for a man to suggest such things was to make him liable to punishment on charges of aggression. We argued that the minority had the right to express itself. Communists in our country express themselves, we reminded him. And then Gennady said—*Gennady* said—that if the Communists were advocating the violent overthrow of a legitimate government, they should not be permitted to exist *because this was not good Marxism.*

Had the Soviet government never been involved in violent revolutionary activity outside of the Soviet Union? we asked.

It had not, Gennady said.

And the heat rose, and the words flew, and the chapters and verse were cited, and all the while Gennady kept laughing at the suggestion that the Soviet Union could have been involved in any attempt to influence the internal affairs of another country.

We discussed the satellites. We went through them one by one and asked whether they had freely elected Communist governments. He said, "Definitely." And I said, "Look, Gennady, there has never been a free election where legitimate alternatives were given." And he said, well, of course, you people don't understand our elections.

What's much more depressing is the manner in which people like Gennady cede their freedom. At lunch that day Gennady said he'd received a letter from his wife in Moscow in four days. Ours had taken twelve to fifteen, and there were some I knew I wasn't getting, because I had cabled word that they'd been sent long before. "Does the address written in English slow it up that much?" Paul said.

"Apparently," said Gennady.

"It takes time to read the letters," I joked. Gennady jolted me with his reply. "That's right." he said.

"Are they still doing that?" I asked. I'd always assumed that they were, but I hadn't expected an admission from a Russian.

"Yes, they are." Gennady said. "They must be. Otherwise your mail would have arrived."

"How do you feel about this?" I asked.

He frowned. "I am against it but unfortunately it is necessary."

"You mean you condone it?" I said.

"More than condone it. I feel it is necessary." He then told us that the government had often found messages written indelibly under regular letters. These the government had actually published in the papers. For this reason he thought it was necessary.

He'd concluded on the basis of my questioning about the individual and society that I was motivated by self-interest, Gennady said now, whereas he was motivated by the interests of society.

I could feel the seams of my temper giving. "The trouble with you bastards is that sometimes you bastards are so goddam smug with your self-righteousness you drive me right up the wall."

"And you with your individual who's better than ours, you're smug too."

"I don't say he's better than yours. I say that what you do deprives him *and* you of his unique gift. I say that we hallow the individual for his uniqueness. And we try to develop his uniqueness as strongly as it can be developed, believing that individuals so developed will produce the highest kind of man, who in turn will build the highest kind of society."

"And so what do you get for your precious individuality? Beatniks. We read about them. They cannot adjust to society. They live useless lives. What kind of society is that?"

"It's the price we pay for principle, that each man must be free to choose. It's his life."

"What is principle?" he said.

"It's something we're willing to defend, even if at times we pay a seemingly irrational price. We've let murderers go to defend principle because the evidence that convicted them was gained unlawfully. The principle is an individual's privacy. If the law permits the privacy of an individual to be invaded in his case, then there is nothing to prevent privacy from being invaded constantly."

This absolutely outraged Gennady. "Common sense tells you that this is ridiculous. The murderers must be punished. Could not the judge stand up and say 'By the authority vested in me in this one case I suspend this right and order the execution of this man?'"

"No."

Gennady could not understand.

There is a final reason why Russians do not react to reality as we might expect them to. *Time* once called it "the persistent vision." Let us look at the world now through the eyes of one who holds it. Let us make the "imaginative leap."

CHAPTER SIX

ALEXEI MARCHUK
A Slightly Clearer View of
a Highly Persistent Vision

We went to the aquatic club on the shore of the lake they call the Bratsk Sea, sat on pier in the sun, and watched the water skiers practice and the kayaks tip and move. Marchuk was there, big shoulders, small eyes, silent for the most part, that faint smile upon his face. We shook hands but he didn't otherwise acknowledge me.

The water was eight degrees centigrade, but when he went under with an aqualung to look for a pair of spectacles a friend had dropped overboard, he wore only brief trunks and a sweater. The younger men, the ones in their early twenties, were heavily muscled, slim-waisted, and supple. The older men, in their thirties, had all developed that first indulgent bulge. All but Marchuk. When his turn to ski came, he got up the first time, skied a hundred yards, kicked off one ski and rode the other out toward the dam. He was not as good as the coach or the champion, Grischa, but he was better than all the others. When he finished, he disappeared to dress, returned in his brown suit, and said in English, "Let's go."

Paul Fusco and I had waited almost two weeks to meet him. Such a legend surrounded him that I'd begun to wonder if he really existed. He'd come to Bratsk straight from Moscow University ten years before. He was only twenty-two then, but the project's chief engineer told him to stop the driving Angara River, if he could. No one else had been able to. Marchuk did, ordering boulders to be dropped one by one from the edge of each bank. Now those boulders lay under the world's largest hydroelectric power station. A Russian journalist had written a story of the exploit, a composer had written a ballad, and all through Russia, for a spell, they had sung the legend of Marchuk. And then Yevtushenko had come and remained for months and written his long poem "The Bratsk Hydroelectric Power Station." Marchuk was the Alexei of that poem.

I'd met him, finally, several days before. Tall, dark, a thick, orderly moustache, high cheekbones, a crew cut, almond-shaped, faintly Mongolian eyes. He was thirty-two, but his manner seemed forty. "We'll talk seriously if you are serious," he said. But he seemed pressed; he was just back from a long trip, and although his desk was bare I sensed that his head was full. I said this probably wasn't the best time for him, and he was grateful. We agreed to meet again.

We met the following Sunday, at a Siberian supper at Rita Nesmelov's house. Her father, Bratsk's ranking economist, was off in Moscow, but you could tell that achievement had its rewards. Half an acre of wooded land and a big, two-story house, old fashioned and roomy.

We ate outdoors under a cupola. Food covered the table: herring, tomatoes, cucumbers sprinkled with dill; onion greens mixed with sour cream; a fruit and vegetable salad; cold tongue; pickled mushrooms; superb little red berries mixed with cranberries; a chopped and creamed radish; meat-balls. After that came hot tongue and a sweet carrot and berry relish; no vodka, cognac instead, and a lot of white wine. Many toasts, the first by Rita's mother, the chunky prototype of mothers everywhere, convinced that we were starving: To peace. To friendship. To the visit of their friends from America. To our missing wives and children. She walked behind the others to come over and clink glasses. Later I raised my glass and said that the American people wanted peace with the Soviet people more than anything in the world; let us drink to the day when you will realize that is true. They were deeply moved and satisfied, and momma came once again to us and crushed our heads to her breasts.

The Marchuks came at last, an hour late. No explanation, just a lot of joking that they would get no cognac. Natasha, his wife, was pretty, with the softness and laughter of a woman in love. They'd just had their third son, and she still showed it around the middle. Marchuk wasted little time; he offered a toast: "We believe our town is a symbol of what we want, peaceful construction."

"To peaceful construction, then," I said, and we drank.

So there was his challenge. It was not antagonistic, but protective, and subtly he was letting me know it. I liked his sharpness and his understated combativeness. He is a proud man, I decided, and a solemn one when the situation warrants. Underneath his laughter, I could feel his thought that this was such a situation. Later, he offered a solemn toast about the responsibility of journalists: They were important to the peace of the world, and they were obliged to report the truth. May they find the strength to report the truth. His eyes were on me. We drank. I asked if I might follow his toast right away. I looked back at him, and said, "To the people who tell the truth."

Laughter. Applause. But not from him. This Marchuk smiled, tipped his glass to me, and drank his wine.

Now, several days later, we drove the long straight street to Alexei's three-room apartment, past the rough-hewn dormitories and office building, the school and auditorium that had been flung up temporarily nine years before. The flat seemed Spartan and worn, yet warm with human presence. There was a rug on the wall, none on the floor. A Renoir print was tacked to another wall. There was a small calendar and near that a small mirror, whose frame held several telegrams. An out-of-tune upright piano hugged a third wall. An old-style victrola sat atop a big buffet. Now Alexei played a Louis Armstrong-Ella Fitzgerald record, which he'd purchased on a recent trip to the States. Then he took out a bottle of vodka. "Would you like some Siberian coffee?" he said with a smile. I declined.

I asked whether what he'd found in the States had corresponded to his expectations. He'd had to introduce several corrections, he replied, but on the whole, expectation and reality had coincided. His greatest disappointment had been the inevitable question "How much do you make?" whenever he tried to talk on major questions. But on the whole, his impressions had been favorable.

Natasha and her mother-in-law, who had come from Moscow to care for the baby, set cakes and plates and two bottles of cold Bulgarian wine onto a small table covered with a tan cloth. As we sipped and ate, I noticed a 32-kilo dumbbell on the floor. I multiplied swiftly: 70.4 pounds. Then I asked Alexei what he did with it. For an answer, he pressed the dumbbell above his head seven times with his right arm.

His first remarks were as Bunyanesque.

"I think the great enthusiasm with which we conduct the settling of this region reflects our faith in humanity. We are the forward line of society. We can very clearly visualize what Siberia means—it means hard currency, diamonds, gold, power, minerals. We very well understand what we are doing for the rest of the country. In 1955 and 1956, people slept in tents. The Chief of Personnel literally slept on a sack with 4,000 letters from people asking to come and help. We didn't have anything. We put on frozen clothing, very often, in the morning. We had to heat our tractors over bonfires to get them started. Our faith in the future is not some empty pronouncement of some utopian society. It's something we built with our own hands."

Did his faith in the future embrace a vision of world communism? I wondered.

"Many of the emerging countries will hesitate about which way they choose to develop," Alexei answered. "We will do everything in our power to convince them that our way is the best."

I asked what he meant by "everything in our power."

"We are just going to work within the confines of our own country to show that our way is the best way for them."

"Is this the extent?" I asked.

"I think this is the major factor of convincing them, and in the future I hope that it would be limited to that, but two sides participate in any game, and if the other side attempts to impose its ideology by force, we will fight."

I asked Alexei whether he realized that I could make the same statement.

"I do," he said. And then: "In any argument, there are three sides—your side, my side, and the right side." And we had a small laugh.

I asked whether the concept he had just outlined implied a change in policy of the Soviet Union.

"Fifty years ago the Soviet Union was preoccupied with its own revolution and couldn't think of anything else."

"And forty, thirty, twenty, and ten years ago?"

"About half of our history has been spent in wars and in reconstruction of the damage caused by wars. We think that ideology can't be imposed by means of violence. That would be fruitless. Marxism has always been against the export of revolution."

I asked whether this held for Lenin, Stalin, and Khrushchev.

"No change," he said. "When a situation is really acute, we allow ourselves to support militarily."

"Are these the so-called 'wars of liberation?' " I asked.

"A war of liberation excludes the possibility of any interference other than moral," he answered. "I don't visualize any violent imposition of our system on the rest of the world."

America remembers Korea, Hungary, the Berlin Wall, the Iron Curtain, the support of Communist parties in other countries culminating in the missile crisis in Cuba. How, I asked, can he rationalize all of these situations with the assertions he had just made?

"I know about that position," he said, "and I have encountered it when I visited your country. I tried to thrash this position out, and I eventually decided it was based on prejudiced information. Our behavior in all these cases was forced on us by the circumstances. We didn't help Castro. The simple truth of the matter is, we have different points of view concerning the same events." Then as an example, he cited the Berlin Wall. Many West Germans had tried to cross to East Berlin in order to escape the draft; twelve hundred had been injured. It was to prevent this that the East Germans had built the wall.

To argue this point now would have defeated my purpose. I could only be struck by the conviction with which he told the story.

"Marx never believed in military Communism," Alexei insisted. "And he was very much against the kind of Communism where everyone was reduced to the same level."

I said, well that brings us to the next great thing that divides us. Which system best develops the individual? I asked him to explain why he felt that his did. He gave three answers.

"One. Individual development depends on the amount of education and the type of education the man gets. In the field of education, in the Soviet Union, he has more opportunity than in the United States where material obstacles often inhibit education.

"Two. Under our system, the individual's participation in the formation of state policy is much greater than in your country. Lenin said that everyone should sometime be a public official. The man's understanding of major political problems makes him more active.

"Three. There is no material obstacle in the way of development of the individual in the arts."

I said I would like to answer these point by point, as an average American would answer.

"One. Your system of education offers a predigested view of knowledge, history, science. We feel that offering the individual a free process—offering him ideas and permitting him to evaluate—develops a questing mind, a skeptical sense, and a free-roving intelligence.

"Two. The political organization of your society does not provide a choice, but only implementation. We feel that for a legitimate democratic choice to exist there must be legitimate alternatives. Your society does not provide them.

"Three. The arts. There may be no material obstacle to the development of an artist, but the content of his work is proscribed."

He sat for a long time. I could hear the breathing of Natasha and his mother across the table. Then he said: "It appears that your average Americans are quite clever."

I asked him what he thought was the major task of Soviet education. He said, "To form an individual capable of deep individual analysis, capable of thinking on his own." But how, I asked, can an individual be capable of free individual analysis if he's offered a unified interpretation of history? "History is a science," he said. "We try to do it objectively. We consider Marxism a science as well. As far as Communist ideology is concerned, you are free to make your choice whether you want to go into that or not."

I then described the fear that had been put into us by the events of Stalin's time. What guarantees were there that hardliners would not once again take power? He answered that the main guarantee was the strengthening of democratic traditions and the presence of collective leadership.

"At what point are affairs private, no matter of concern for the state?" I asked then.

He thought for a long time, with his head bowed. Then he looked up and said, "My family, my personal belongings, my freedom of choice of a job, my freedom and choice of hobbies."

"And the freedom to emigrate?" I asked. I got no answer. "And freedom of speech?"

"Absolutely."

"And freedom to strike?"

"We have no laws that forbid the right to strike. You are raising questions that we never consider because we never have these problems."

I asked whether he believed everything he read in his newspapers. He said, "Yes, we do believe what is published, but that doesn't exclude the need for independent analysis and approach." I asked if he had opportunity for such analysis, and he said he did—that he could always read U.S. papers. *"The New York Times* is in our library and I can listen to the Voice of America. On that basis, I can make up my mind." I asked if he listened to the "Voice" and he said he did. I asked if he ever read *The New York Times,* and he said that he really didn't, that he lacked the time, but he was consoled by his access to it. I scored one point for his honesty.

I put my notebook away to indicate that we were through for the night. Alexei smiled, warmly now, and said a few nice things. Natasha and his mother settled back, almost in relief. Outside, the light was fragile. I was tired. I asked Alexei if I could sample some of that Siberian coffee he'd shown me earlier. It was 100-proof vodka and we drank it without breathing so as not to burn our throats.

The following day, we drove to the dam. It was to be officially dedicated at ceremonies that fall, and now they were all forcing the pace. Marchuk flew about, vaulting fences, dropping down ladders on the face of the dam, looking through cracks. Imagine what this man must feel, I thought. He built this thing. There'd been several thousand engineers, but he'd been one of the keys.

As he got out of the car, I told him how sorry I was that we had no place to invite him. We would like to take him to dinner. He said he could bring Natasha to the Intourist restaurant if we liked. I raced back to my room to review the notes of the night before and go over some of the questions

I'd postponed asking. By the time I had finished he and Natasha were already walking to the restaurant.

During dinner, they told us about themselves. They'd met in the same hydroelectric engineering class at college in Moscow; she was the union organizer who loved to coax her classmates out of lectures and to the cinema; he was the serious *Komsomol* youth leader. When they fell in love, the choice of a place to work became urgent. Each college-trained student must go for three years to someplace mutually agreeable to him and a special commission. Separation of newly-weds is not uncommon. Alexei wanted Bratsk; specialists were rare; he knew he would get responsible work; he liked Siberia; he considered himself a Siberian (born in Omsk); he loved hiking. He convinced Natasha, then to be sure, listened through a crack in the door when she talked to the commission. Her father was an important man; the commission members knew him and tried to discourage her: insects, crude living, cold. Why not graduate study in Moscow? She insisted. Alexei and Natasha married that summer and came to Bratsk.

We spoke of our children. Did the Marchuks ever imagine a conflict between society's ideas about child-raising, and parents'? They couldn't imagine such a conflict.

I said that one of my goals as a parent was to try to raise my children to make up their own mind and resist the pressures of their peers. Natasha said she wanted that for their children too.

I asked whether that couldn't produce a conflict. Society says the individual should agree. I recalled the verdict of the young school girl; if a person didn't go along with the majority, he should be "re-educated."

"I think that girl was just too young," Natasha said. "I

don't consider the decision of the majority as obligating. It doesn't suppress the individual. It doesn't mean he can't maintain his views." Alexei agreed, in principle, but he felt the minority should conform, or go along, after it had had a chance to express its views.

"Why are you asking all these questions about individuality?" Natasha asked then. "Do you think that our society creates a group of people who all think alike?"

"The individual's resilience is a critical political factor," I answered, "It establishes to what extent he will permit society to invade his rights. If he permits it, the consequence is totalitarianism. What we came here to learn is whether there was sufficient resilience to resist a slide back to dictatorship of the Stalinist type if the threat should ever materialize again."

In the evening, the Marchuk residence. Bohemia glass from Czechoslovakia, a ruby red with gold design, the label still on, and christened now with champagne. Long pauses before answering questions.

His father entered the party in 1942, at the front. He was senior physician of a regiment and later of a medical battalion. His parents, both doctors, had wanted him to study medicine, and it had been "quite a job to wriggle out" of pressures.

He'd been influenced by the *Komsomol,* the Communist youth organization, which he'd entered in 1948. *Komsomol* members had been an example at the school where he studied. They'd helped an old woman whose husband had perished in the war. They'd helped in factories. They were dynamic people. He wanted to become an "in" person.

He joined the Communist party in 1960 in Bratsk. "By that time I felt mature enough to choose the general line of my life, the ideology. Generally, the time between 1953 and 1960 was very interesting. I witnessed with my own eyes the birth of a country, a period when a huge and severe country came to be utilized. I witnessed how 600 Communists worked; they were among the workers constructing a high-power grid from Irkutsk to Bratsk. Before making my decision I thought about it a lot, especially in view of the facts revealed after the death of Stalin."

The crucial event had been a brawl in 1959, in which his best friend was fatally mauled. The friend had been seeing his girl home. Four drunks accosted them; he told them off. After he had taken the girl home, he returned and they jumped him. He was rushed to the hospital, but it was too late. "We found the persons," Marchuk said. "Two had served prison terms. These were the days when we had exemplary court sessions. We tried them and the final sentence was death for the ringleader.

"The incident shocked us. It made us all feel that we were responsible, not just for the industrial complex, but for the life, for the morals of the people who lived around us. At the time, I was the secretary of the local *Komsomol* organization. We determined that we must help people organize the second half of their day. You must understand that the population here was variegated. When the fame of Bratsk first spread all kinds of people came here for the 'long ruble.' Whole groups used to come, like a brigade of sailors that had just been discharged. Frequently there would be clashes at the dance halls between these groups. We would isolate these people and tell them how we visualized Bratsk. We had to sift and isolate the hostile elements in our community. We wanted to become the real guiding light. For three years I headed this *Komsomol* group in its organization of the second half of the day."

I asked him then about Stalin.

"The exposure of the cult of the personality had come to us as a heavy blow," he replied "You must understand that we hadn't known anything about the deviation from the straight line. Stalin's brains had played a big part in winning the war. I asked myself, was it necessary or would it have been better without the revelations? I found the answer in 1956 on the road to Bratsk. From the window of our carriage we saw a labor camp. It had rusted barbed wire and watchtowers. I could understand then how hard it must have been for those people to stay there without feeling in any way guilty."

"What's to prevent it from happening again?" I asked.

"You want too much of me," he said. "I didn't enter the Party to see that this wouldn't happen again. I think that the reestablishment of our democratic traditions is the guarantee that it won't happen again. It serves as an example. It cautioned people. Valuable lessons are sometimes learned from mistakes. I'm quite sure that no repetition is going to happen again."

I asked him if he would tell me what a Communist of his generation believed.

"I like the question," he replied. "I want to answer. I want to think about it." He laughed. "I promise you I won't consult the Central Committee of the Party."

We met again the next evening at the Ungada Culture House. Marchuk started right in.

"The first thing I believe is in the correctness of our teachings which we call Marxist-Leninist. This is not fanaticism, this is not blind faith. This belief of mine finds support in the following factors. In 1848 when the Communist Manifesto was written by Karl Marx, Communism appeared as a specter to which no one paid any attention. When the Communists took one-sixth of this globe, they did it with only 340,000 members. Today the Communists number millions, their force is something tangible in the life of the world.

"My conviction grew and strengthened due to the severe test the country underwent in the Second World War, and in the emergence of a number of young independent states which try to choose a noncapitalist road of development. I believe in the collective ideal. I believe in the economic might of our country, which has been established since 1917. In 1917 one couldn't imagine a discussion like we're having now, a discussion among equals.

"Finally, we are trying to shape up a new man. Today, I thought a lot not on the question you have put to me but about your particular anxiety to jealously guard the right of the individual, which you seem to feel is being imposed upon by society. With us this conflict is impossible because basically the interests coincide. The old concept of my 'home is my fortress' is too narrow for us. Our man has outgrown it; he is prepared to give a big part of his life to society. His personal and his public life interrelate.

"If you are not too tired of my stories I will tell you another one. In 1961 we were constructing the bottom orifices of a tunnel. They were 100 meters long, the side of the opening was ten by twelve meters. They are closed by metal shields. In one of these tunnels the workers saw a crack. They reported the accident to the chief engineer. He went to the tunnel personally. It wasn't necessary for him to go down. He was quite elderly and he was very distinguished and honored, but his personal presence was of great psychological importance. The others wanted to follow him.

"It was an empty, dark tunnel. Very silent, water dripping. He examined the metal shield. Then he called his associate over. He said, 'Comrade, my experience prompts only one decision. You must pour a concrete plug. I cannot give you any guarantee that it won't burst. The only assurance I can give is that I and the engineers will be present. I can only suggest that the faster you work the better it is. Only volunteers should do this work.'

"The whole team of concrete pourers volunteered. They stayed on the job for forty-eight hours. Their meals were sent in. They stayed until the danger ended."

Alexei paused, looked at the floor, then at me. "I believe in my tomorrows," he said. "I believe our material possibilities are better. I believe there is a possibility for greater spiritual life. I believe we will be able to fulfill the goals we have set for ourselves. I believe that the world is not going to know any terrible, devastating war. I believe our society is more fair and just. I believe this because I have seen a Bowery Street in America."

Four dismaying and dangerous years have passed since that encounter with Alexei. In that short time, some of the best minds in the Soviet Union have been enclosed in jails or asylums, or encased in the vastness of exile. In the name of socialism, those ingrained Russian attributes—the maddening claim to infallibility, the provocative faith in some future destiny, the suffocating demand for conformity—have found new vigor at home and inevitably affected the world. What George Kennan also said of the Soviet Union in 1967, in his article for *Foreign Affairs,* had been more than revalidated by 1971. "External relations," he wrote, "are still troubled and made precarious by the neurotic view the regime takes of itself as a government among governments, by its predilection for secrecy and mystification in method, by its addiction to the use of exaggeration and falsehood in political utterance, by its persecution mania and its pathological preoccupation with espionage, by its excessive timidity and suspicion . . . about personal contacts between Soviet citizens and foreigners, by the inordinate role it concedes to its secret police apparatus in the conduct of its foreign policy."

As the voices of protest were stilled, as the Russian tanks clanked into Prague, as the Kremlin surreptitiously wired a Middle East explosion while thunderously denouncing others' equally deplorable acts, my thoughts increasingly visited Alexei. I yearned to be in his home once again, asking, "What now of your 'reestablishment of democratic traditions,' your noninterference in the affairs of other states, your peaceful competition?"

His answer, I am sure, would have been naïve, unsatisfying, even infuriating. And yet it would have been invaluable to an understanding of the mainstream of Russian life. For that life, a blend of contradictions, is carried around in the likes of an Alexei Marchuk, believing because he has been trained to, because psychologically he needs to, because patriotically he wants to, because—and this is so important—he persists in his vision that socialism can ultimately provide the most beneficial setting for man.

He believes this because he has seen a "Bowery Street"; because his history books tell him that most Russians were serfs before the Revolution, and that the armies of the West, including the United States, assisted a counterrevolution against the Bolsheviks; because he has seen his country develop, and his own life has been spiritually enriched in the process. He believes that any underdeveloped country can succeed by utilizing the same system. But he knows, because he is told, that there are political impediments. The ruling classes in rich countries don't want to lose wealth or power. Neither did his Czar. (No mention is made of Stalin.) These ruling classes are assisted by the United States, which wishes all underdeveloped countries to remain cheap-labor suppliers of inexpensive raw materials that can then be sold back as expensive finished products to those very ruling classes, as well as the bourgeoisie. Alexei interprets all international events in these terms, and because of that, he blames us for the Cold War. No argument will persuade him otherwise.

He will give his leaders the benefit of every doubt, and believe what he is told. If those prison camps begin to fill again, he will worry, ask questions, argue, and even protest. But he will not revolt.

So truth in Russia may well be "round" to the extent that Russians like Alexei do not react to events as the events themselves would make us think they would. But if truth is round, it is also bleak, and what good is *that* kind of truth?

I don't believe it is all that bleak.

I think there is a further element of the truth that must be added to the absence of objective critical judgment as we define it, to the repression of intellectuals, and to the indifference and acquiescence of the masses. My own experience persuades me that a more rational factor exists within the Soviet Union today than, given the historical framework, we have any reason to expect. This "factor" is the sum of several elements that are the natural yield of change.

Neo-Stalinism is a part of the truth in Russia today. What preceded this retreat, and still exists, is another part of the truth. These contradictory elements must be fitted together before truth itself is complete.

What has gone before does not satisfy our Western sense of what ought to be. It is a hopeful reality because it represents something better than what was.

Despite the dot of current news, the roundness of current history reveals a pattern of change to accommodate what the Communists have learned about man. That the Russians may turn back in fright from such knowledge is disappointing and understandable, but not necessarily final. At some point, this knowledge assumes a life of its own to which Russia's leaders must eventually respond.

That life, too, is carried around in the likes of an Alexei Marchuk. It is the one aspect of his existence in which the persistent vision cannot be fogged. It demands that this vision mature into a good life for those who view the world through its prism.

Alexei requires improvements, not so much to increase his comforts as to sustain his beliefs. To sustain those beliefs requires changes—powerful changes that however halting, however given to periods of retreat, can never be wholly undone.

CHAPTER SEVEN

NUDGING RIGHTWARD

Political designations in Communist countries are as multiple and variable as combinations of weather. In tracking them, it is helpful to remember that fundamentally they are like seasons in the Southern Hemisphere—the exact reverse of our own. Thus a "leftist" is one who believes in orthodoxy and in corollary authoritarian force to implement it. A "rightist" is one who believes in "reactionary" ideas like bourgeois democracy and revision.

The four years since Russia's fiftieth anniversary celebration have seen a perceptible move leftward in the direction of an earlier orthodoxy. But compared to its violent birth and nightmarish formation, the System has nudged to the right.

What Russian communism set out to do and what it has achieved are not the same thing. Then it was "From each according to his abilities, to each according to his needs." Now, the suggestion that they ever considered a classless society is described as "another bourgeois lie." Then, sacrifice was the sole virtue, and the collective ideal dominated life. Now, pleasure is acceptable, and the Age of the Individual is near. Now, the Russians talk about revamping their educational system because the present one kills initiative. They are marshaling hundreds of social scientists and thousands of data collectors in a long-range project to bridge the gap between aspiration and reality for Soviet man. Bonuses, profit sharing, incentive pay, personal possessions, all once frowned on by Marxist purists, are now justified with a logic that bewilders Western visitors. The Marxist-Leninists today use the literature of their gods as a bigot uses the Bible: they extract statements out of context to prove the point needing proof. "One should never take Marx or Lenin literally," a social scientist suggests. "They should be elaborated in accordance with the present situation." What the Marxists will not acknowledge is that in their fundamental assumption about man, Marx and Lenin were wrong. Both believed that people raised in a Socialist environment would be selfless. The current love affair with profit is just one of many oblique concessions that ego cannot be subdued.

One warm Sunday afternoon a few years ago, I strolled down Moscow's Gorki Street and stepped into a taxi, placing my feet carefully on top of two young Russian bodies. For half an hour, the taxi drove a rambling route, stopping at last at an apartment building on the outskirts of the city. The two young Russians then took me to the room of a friend.

He was sturdy, handsome, fresh-faced. His hair was neatly cut. He wore an American-made button-down sport shirt. The walls of his room were covered with American mementos—college pennants, record covers, sketches of jazz heroes, a tiny American flag, a John F. Kennedy button, even a flattened carton of Philip Morris.

"I am very disloyal," he said. "I think the politics of my country is very heavy, very wrong. I want to live in the United States. I'm followed all the time. All the time, propaganda. The most important thing for me is freedom, liberty, to meet foreign people, to go to Europe and America, but

I cannot do it. Life here is terrible. I cannot live here. Everyone feels the way I do."

"He's wrong," the second boy said. "We *can* live here. We must stay here and study. When I graduate from the university, I will have a good job, earn good money, raise my family. Progress is good. Everyone feels the way I do. They want a little more freedom, and that's all."

The third smiled. "They're both wrong," he said. "Those two are not fighters. I am a fighter. I'm in complete accord with Lenin's ideas, but our government has changed many things. We must return to those ideas. Now, there is no chance. In twenty years, when everyone has a good job, we'll have our chance. Almost everyone feels the way I do."

There is no way, in the Soviet Union, of attaching scientific percentages to each of these views. What can be confirmed is that all three exist; what can be suggested is what each signifies.

The first young man represents the small group of Soviet youth that, either for ideological or practical reasons, cannot get along. It is defiant and usually in trouble. Its ranks include the "hooligans" who so outrage Soviet authorities and make the headlines. The second young man represents the largest group—docile, bland, unsophisticated, accepting with pleasure the numerous offerings of Soviet life, needing frequent reassurance that "progress is good." The third young man represents the exciting dynamic in Soviet life today—a sizable minority of youth who are critical, well-educated, and shrewd. They make no scenes, but exert steady pressure. They are both an affirmation of and force for change.

"These Russian kids are a kind of miracle," one who knows them well told me a few years ago, "vivid, alert, curious, open-minded, friendly, and almost completely uncontaminated by the heritage of Stalinist cynicism. I don't think they take the political or cultural pretensions of the current leadership seriously and yet they are not all 'apolitical.' What they sense, above all, is the backwardness of the system under which they live."

They find propaganda square. They may daydream through Marxist lectures or hoot down party polemicists. They are as contemptuous of Red Chinese Stalinism as they are of our presence in Vietnam. Their great contempt at home, according to Vladimir Lisovsky, a Leningrad sociologist, who specializes in their problems, is reserved for dishonesty, red tape, careerism, bureaucracy—a sure sign, says Lisovsky, of sensitivity to the manner in which their lives are governed. Where his generation, raised under Stalin, accepted ideas on faith, this generation accepts nothing without investigation. "The difference has produced an authority clash. The fathers are used to getting the word. The sons don't have the same attitude toward authority. Parents try to force their children to accept their views without any criticism. The kids disagree. They want to lead their own lives."

This generation's great difference from the last is found in the role that each concedes the individual. The older generation grew up with the idea that the individual had no rights. The state was everything; no sacrifice was too great; indulgence was sin; ends justified the means. This generation believes that the individual has the right to a decent life. Pleasure is not sin; freedoms should be increased; travel should be possible. "To our next meeting," a young engineer proposed, his vodka glass raised, "not in Moscow, but somewhere else—New York or Chicago or San Francisco or London or Paris."

"When I was a child," an old professor reminisces, "it was downright indecent for me to say I wanted a decent flat or a car or good clothes. My preoccupation was the world revolution, the overthrow of capitalism. To think of anything else was inconceivable, unethical. I don't say the young man today doesn't care about revolution. But the modern view is that the human being has the right to be happy as a human being, as an individual. In my day, we could be happy only when we were sacrificing our lives."

Soviet youth are for socialism, but without political impediments or party capriciousness. "They want to compare ideas and systems for themselves, and not have somebody else do it for them," an American studying in Leningrad told me. "Some people feel that if they took a good look at the West, they'd decide for it. That's not true. They'd still take their own system."

They are critical of this system, but not cynical about it; dissatisfied, but not disillusioned. And so incapable at times of admitting their own humanness. One day I'd questioned the editors of a youth paper in Leningrad, only to be scolded after some minutes by the ranking editor, easily fifteen years my junior. "By the nature of your questions, it's obvious that you don't understand Soviet youth," he said. I had been asking about the interest of youth in the good life, when everyone knew that youth was dedicated to the building of communism. There followed a tumultuous exchange. But when we finished, the editor asked if I would answer a question of his. "Tell me," he began, "quite apart from political matters, how does the Soviet Union strike you from the point of view of our conditions, our apartments and our transportation. Does it seem to you that a person can live well here?"

In Russia today, that is the preoccupying question. It is also the key to change.

A centralized economy works adequately in the initial states of industrialization or in times of emergency when there is so much to be produced that mistakes can be absorbed, and when sacrifice is considered the normal response to the times. But a people not living in heroic times will not respond heroically; the need is simply not there. At that point a monolithic society must refine its economy in a series of specific ways. To move into a new economic society requires new uses for individual men—and a revision of approaches to them.

One illustration of the change is found in the work begun in 1967 by Gennady Ossipov, then president of the Soviet Sociological Association. A small, sturdy, square-jawed, and terribly serious young man, Ossipov had organized a research project engaging 120 scientists, 200 assistants, and several thousand data collectors for a three- to four-year period. Its title: The Social and Social-Psychological Problems of Economic Reform. The study arose because of concern over the overweighting of aspiration, which creates dissatisfaction when unfulfilled. The result: depression of productivity. "The dissatisfaction of even one worker influences others whose aspirations are not in contradiction with their work," Ossipov told me in his university office one day. The state should orient the individual "in conformity with reality." It was doing so now on the basis of recommendations of the sociologists. Had the state been derelict in previous times? Ossipov sighed: "It was one of thousands of factors."

The first task of the revolution, he said, had been to build industry, clothe people, develop the economy. The second task had been to rebuild after the devastation of World War II. Now at last, the Russians could attend to the precise needs of man—his "delicate" problems, his stimuli, his relationships.

Ossipov insisted that the problems were not products of dissatisfaction, but simply the logical aftermath of the first and second tasks of the revolution. Before, the requirements of the individual had been minimal, he said. Now the situation had changed. Now, they could ask industry to concern itself with man: labor organization, community relations, labor-management relations, awards, conditions, alienation. "Interpersonal relations become a more important factor as you get into phase three," he said. "Certain violence to interpersonal relations kept us from what we should have had. In the U.S. you took the social-psychological factors into account and got more productivity."

"Which are you changing?" I asked, "aspiration or reality?"

He laughed, then answered. "Eighty percent of young people queried want to be astronauts or scientists. Obviously, the need here is to change aspiration. To change aspiration you have to get into education."

And economics.

Soviet economic reform came into being in 1965 because the economy was displaying all the symptoms of overcentralization—diminished output and profit, increasing stockpiles, a scarcity of resources to devote to goods that people really wanted.

Following a prolonged debate, the Russians decided to decentralize—placing control, wherever possible, at the local level, offering incentives for improved performance.

The results were soon apparent. One factory that had worked at a loss until 1966, reported more than $1 million in profit at the time of my 1967 visit. "The workers are highly interested in their share," a foreman told me. They'd reorganized, worked harder, tried new methods, introduced new machinery. A number of jobs had been eliminated. In its first year under the new system, the factory had paid average bonuses of $55 a month, about 25 percent of an average salary, to more than 1,500 of its 3,800 workers.

By June, 1969, according to the Russians, 33,600 industrial enterprises had gone over to the new system. These enterprises accounted for 80 percent of the country's industrial output and 90 percent of its profit. The Russians maintained that factory profits had risen between 15 and 20 percent annually. Numerous internal and technical problems had been encountered—most significant among them, the reluctance of central planners to cede their power or abandon old habits—but the remedy in almost every case was to further the cause through profit inducements and "bonus incentive" funds.

"Little by little," notes economist Alexander Birman, "the sociological procedures and methods used in production planning and management are being extended and improved. The result will be a considerable growth in production efficiency and hence an improved standard of living."

The result will be—and is already—a good deal more than that. Once you begin to search for economic answers in the form of decentralized answers, you must begin to permit men to think for themselves and make their own decisions.

The political impact of this process is the most critical factor now at work in the Communist world.

The people who run socialist countries are tinkering with economic devices and discarding what doesn't work. This is a slow process, but an inevitable one because countries must do it or starve; it leads irresistibly toward more universal ideas about man—what he wants and what he is and what makes him function better. Its pace varies from country to country, but that has more to do with national disposition than depths of dogmatic conviction.

This process has caused enormous changes already, and will cause a good many more. It explains the promise and the heartbreak that characterize, simultaneously, socialism's slow movement rightward today.

Let us look at heartbreak first.

They are said to be a minor people. Their national story is brief, disruptive, sad. Their literary hero is a canny bumbler who perennially outwits faceless Kafkaesque bureaucrats. Once, one of their reformers tried to unite Christendom and was burned for his troubles. To present-day Czechs and Slovaks, he served more as object lesson than inspiration —almost as if they knew what was coming. Bitter memories reinforced their taste for compromise. "This word means something else in your society than it does in ours," said a man of Prague. "Is it a compromise to go against tanks with your fists?" Yet, in one of those bizarre happenstances on which history sometimes pivots, these same careful Czechs and Slovaks loosed an idea so extraordinary it convulsed the Communist world—that freedom and socialism could join.

Economically, the state was to exercise a "social power" over the marketplace, but the market itself was to be free. Politically, the Communist party was to assume a fatherly role in affairs of state and seek popular sanction at the polls. Ideologically, men might organize, or protest, or leave if they wished. The venom of repression that had poisoned socialism everywhere would have been gone at last from here.

The emotions aroused by Czechoslovakia's golden spring have badly blurred its origins, and quite possibly its lesson. The Czechoslovakian adventure did not begin as a grasp for liberty, nor even a gesture against the Soviet Union. Until August, 1968, Czechoslovakia was the closest the Russians came to having a satellite friend. In 1946, the Czech Communist party polled 38 percent of the vote in free elections; even in 1948, when the Communists' thrust for power had been fully consolidated, 75 percent of Czechoslovaks could still be considered prosocialist. But the twenty-year interval had taught them a bitter practical lesson. The impetus of their quest for democratic socialism was economic. They wished to infuse individual energy into an authoritarian system that hadn't worked for them.

Long after other socialist bloc countries had taken their cue from Nikita Khrushchev and begun to experiment with their economies, Czechoslovakia remained rigidly traditional. By 1966, the most highly industrialized of all the socialist countries had fallen into disrepair; the most advanced economy in the bloc was providing less of a living standard than Poland or Hungary. Shortages were widespread. Exports were falling. Czechoslovakia must export to live, but her industries were no longer producing goods that were competitive in price and quality on the world market. Bureaucrats ground out their quotas oblivious or impervious to what was going on around them. When, in June, 1966, the thirteenth congress of the Czech Communist party agreed to introduce a radically new policy, the job was handed to an economist named Ota Sik.

A lifelong Communist, Professor Sik had studied other socialist systems, particularly the reforms of Libermann, the Russian economist. What Sik now proposed was to relate production to demand by decentralizing the operation of the economy. The idea had a compelling paper logic, but the moment Sik tried to apply it to reality, he encountered trouble. A decentralized economy and a highly centralized political structure are contradictions in terms; the first implies change that threatens the second.

President Novotny and his group knew that the new politics would mean sacrifice for the workers who formed the base of their political power. Some nonrational industries might have to shut down; this meant unemployment for the workers—as well as for some of the party functionaries. Once again, the powers throttled Sik.

But late in 1967 a series of events loosened Novotny's grip—a writers' protest, a student rebellion, and finally a scandal involving a general officer closely connected to the President. Leonid Brehznev came to Prague to rescue his man; he succeeded only in postponing the inevitable. By January, 1968, Novotny had lost his top party post, and would soon lose the presidency. Sik was free to move.

I saw him in Prague five months later. We sat in soft chairs in a corner of his cavernous office, his desk far off in the diagonal corner, a portrait of Lenin behind it. Small, rather pleasant oils, landscapes, all but lost, hung on each immense wall. Sik had survived four years of a German concentration camp; he was forty-nine now; twice that year, he had been seriously ill. Yet he looked marvelous and he was working, he told me, fourteen to sixteen hours a day. For the next hour, as I questioned him, Ota Sik blueprinted his new economic society—which differed significantly in degree from the Soviet model. What follow are the pertinent highlights.

"We want to stay on a socialist basis," Sik explained, "but a completely different type of socialist society from that which has been developing here up until now. The decisive fact is that we are doing away with strict centralized planning. We are preserving certain types of macroeconomic planning, but only as a basis for economic policies of the government. The main thing is to plan—for five, ten, fifteen years—the aims of economic development for the country. We want simply to inform the companies about these aims, but they will be free to make their own policy within the factories."

"But the nature of the factory—its social function—will be predetermined, will it not?"

"The socialist nature of these companies is established by common ownership."

"But the choice of product, the allocation of resources, will remain an affair of the state, will it not?"

"It will go over to the companies."

"All of it?"

"The only difference will be that surplus will not go to individual shareholders, but will go instead to government in form of pre-set taxes. Part goes to the state, while the rest goes to the company."

"Which brings us to the problem of incentives. You *will* structure a system of incentives?"

"The profit pie would be cut in three slices—the state taking some as a form of taxation, the enterprise taking some for reinvestment, and the workers taking the remainder as a bonus."

"In your reform program, you said, 'It is not possible to blunt permanently economic policy by taking from those who work well and giving to those who work badly. Therefore it is necessary to objectivize value relations.' What in fact does this mean and how will it work?"

The problems, Sik explained, had been caused by loans from the state to enterprises that weren't profitable. "That meant taking away from those enterprises that were profitable.

"Marx spoke only of doing away with private ownership of the means of production. But there's no word about doing away with material interest. In the Soviet Union, they have created social ownership that disregards the material interest. They do recognize the material interest of the workers, but not the material interest of the company, or the factory. They supposed that it was enough to decide centrally the production of a factory and then make the worker materially interested in the plan. But that's a mistake, because nobody in the center can replace world market demands. In the past, the aim was only to fulfill the plans, only the quantity of production, and for this we didn't need to have differences between the wages. The plan required growth of brute production, and didn't make any requirements regarding quality. In the first years after the war, it was enough to build more and more factories and employ more and more workers, and to increase production all the time. But at a certain moment, people needed different new products. In the competition with the West, they needed greater technical quality of the products. Then it wasn't enough, this centralized planning from above stressing quantity. It needed something from below: quality."

"You're suggesting not only was it not good economics, it wasn't good Marx."

"Marx didn't go into detail. He simply said that the means of production has to be socialized. Marx speaks about liberating man not only from economic but political oppression. That is what we forgot in the past. We had liberated man from economic oppression but not from political and all the other human oppressions. It was a system that had no economic exploitation, but we forgot about the political. It was a system of personal power."

The deeper one probed in Prague through that spring, the more utterly convinced he became that the Czechoslovaks meant what they said on two critical points: everything they proposed to achieve would be achieved within the framework of socialism. Not for a moment did they consider leaving the Soviet bloc. History cannot be undone, they kept saying; they had lived now as Socialists for twenty years; their workers did not want factories returned to private hands; it was too late for the farmers to go back to their old ways, and their children had moved away. Munich, when England sold them out to Hitler, in 1938, taught them they could not rely on the West. An editor said coldly, "There is no reality for us severed from the Soviet Union." Why, then, did the Russians move in?

In Moscow, the following summer, an editor of *Pravda* would respond to the same question by stalking to an office wall and shouting, "Here, look at the map!" He would argue that Czechoslovakia, whose borders touched the West, could not be lost. That, he said, would have been bad for both sides; it would have upset the balance of power.

But the answer thrusts far beyond the mortal issue of collective security. It settles ultimately on the gravest issue of all—the Marxists' view of man.

The Russians say man's nature requires forceful shaping. The Czechoslovaks were saying it doesn't. The Russians say man is incapable of serving a socialist state until social pressure has molded his thought. The Czechoslovaks were saying communism must justify itself in a free democratic process. The Russians say the class struggle must be relentlessly pursued. The Czechoslovaks maintained it had ended. "It's possible," said an economist, "that repressive measures are essential at the outset in the socializing of a society. But are these repressive measures essential to socialism? We're announcing that they're not." The Russians, whose past is one of almost total repression, felt otherwise.

Russians mistrust everyone, most of all themselves. They have never known democracy; the Czechs had known it well. The Russians believe that their methods are certain and the reformers' methods are not. What frightened the Russians most of all was that the Marxist ideas they had forsaken Czechoslovakia's Marxists had seized. In a half-articulated and often fumbling way, the thinkers in Prague were groping for a utopian vision embedded in the writings of young Karl Marx: the state should exist for the individual, not the individual for the state.

"Marx wanted a society in which the positive aspects of personality could be developed and the negative discouraged," said philosopher Karel Kosik. History's quarrel with the Marxists is that the idea has never worked. But Prague's reformers in 1967–68 were arguing essentially that Communists had always fallen back on Lenin's authoritarian devices and forsaken Marx's humanistic ideals. "The kind of socialism presented here twenty years ago was nothing more than state capitalism from the last century," said a young Prague student. "I'm not against socialism at all. The old generation took the idea on faith. I would like to take it rationally. We are not arguing against the aim or the task. We are arguing only about means."

The Czechoslovaks were not certain they could succeed, but they very much wanted to try. "This country should try to find out whether something called democratic socialism is possible," said one forthright writer, Antonin Liehm, before the invasion. "We feel it should be possible. Maybe we'll show it's not possible. Maybe we'll show that what we call socialism cannot be democratic. Or maybe it will be democratic, but no longer what we call socialism. We have to find out. We're having an experience that nobody before Czechoslovakia has known."

It was an experience the Russians would not risk, and so they and their friends went in.

As the Warsaw Pact tanks crossed the Czech and Slovak borders, *Look's* Chicago presses were printing a lead article of mine, called "Last Try for Utopia." Chance had put me that night in New York. I hurried to the editorial offices to rewrite the story. My first act was to change the title to "Lament for a Lost Revolution."

It's possible that my first reaction was right. It was certainly right then. And the time since has offered no material contradiction. In 1968, liberal Alexander Dubcek would have won an honest election. Today, Dubcek is cashiered from the Communist party; the conservative government that replaced his reformers is almost totally without support. "One thing it absolutely cannot do," says a witness, "it cannot produce a nail." Czechoslovakia today is a wreck.

It is tempting to seize the fate of the heartbroken Dubcek as a metaphor of world communism's future. It's possible that the exercise is apt. It's equally possible that it is self-deluding and dangerous. No single moment or solitary event can support a historical judgment; all the clues must be entered before the judgment is cast.

Let's examine a major one now.

A nervous vigor pervaded Budapest in the autumn of 1956. That Tuesday evening, public meetings were under way all over town; every few minutes, the roar of an approving audience rent the air. In the streets of Pest, a swelling crowd of young Hungarians, heady from a day of protests, marched on the government's radio station to broadcast demands for reforms. The first of these: withdrawal of Soviet troops. At the station, a delegation went inside—and was promptly arrested by the political police. Sensing their leaders' fate, the crowd pressed forward. Edgy police opened fire. A demonstrator fell dead. With that, the crowd stormed the station; an hour later, the ground floor was theirs. So began the worst clash ever within the Communist world: first, Hungarian against Hungarian; then, Hungarian against Russian. In thirteen days, the Revolution of 1956 was over, its instigators physically and spiritually crushed.

Ten years after that revolution, the people of Budapest challenged belief. Not only had they buried their memories, they offered a startling example of what European communism could provide and where it might be heading. They had softened the system, and tamed it to their purpose. They were irreverent of doctrine, wryly humorous, and cautiously hopeful. Not all of them had what they wanted, but life was so much better that they were willing to settle for something less than what they once demanded. They were tired of struggle; they had discarded illusion; they wanted to enjoy life now.

If 1956 taught the Soviet Union that Hungary required autonomy, that where Russians take comfort in the swaddlings of suspicion, Hungarians are outgoing and gregarious, it also taught the Hungarians that they would live and die in the Soviet orbit, and would just have to make the best of it. They had done precisely this. They had accepted the framework of socialism, but within this framework, they were increasingly free. They tinkered. They changed. Slowly, surely, they were spicing life to their taste.

The only visible reminder of Soviet style in Budapest by 1966 was the red star that adorned government buildings and efficient factories. Otherwise, one blinked. Restaurants were crowded, tables laden. Deft headwaiters flamed meats and crepes. Schmaltzy violinists bent over pampered ladies. Mornings, afternoons, evenings, the people of Budapest

flocked to their coffeehouses, the elite in clothes by Clara
Rothschild, the masses in well-fashioned goods. Or, undressed
to the minimum, they sunned and bathed at baroque, gar-
gantuan pools.

Budapest had always been exuberant. Its life was dialogue; its melancholy political history, the bursts of inhumanity by its villains, failed to quench its heroes. Its people
were affectionate, eager, open, relaxed, urbane, witty. They
still were, but with a difference. Now, they moved quietly,
separately, suppressing passion. A riddle explained the change:
"Why is socialism like your wife?" Answer: "That which we
have, we must love." It was not love, it was an arrangement.
As a theater director said, "To be or not to be is not the
question. It is. There are no people waiting for a change.
This is our life." A young intellectual declared, "No one
would go to the streets today." Even the Freedom fighters,
who led the revolution, had been absorbed into the society.
"It's all over," said an observer. "They've made their peace
with the regime."

Were they satisfied? "No," said one Hungarian. "But
that doesn't mean we're against. It doesn't mean that we
want something different. What we want is to perfect what
we have."

Were they free? No, not in the Western sense, but so
much freer than they were that almost no one seemed to
mind. "In the early '50s, everybody had to read the party
newspaper every morning and officially declare his approval
of what it said. This was insupportable, really," a writer recalled. "Today, if you don't want to read the paper, you
don't. Nobody forces you. Nobody asks your opinion. We
cultivate our own garden."

"Are you a Communist is not such an important question now," a non-Communist said. "Are you a Communist?"

a young man asked his girl in a film. "Yes," she said. "And you?"

"I'm an engineer," he replied.

A diplomat remembered when purists would say, "She can't be a Communist. She paints her nails." The diplomat, a Communist, and a lady, smiled: "When you think back on that," she said, "it's with a sigh of relief."

The most heartening aspect of life in Budapest ten years after the Revolution of 1956 was the freedom of its intellectuals to address life in realistic terms. Nothing was spared, not even the System. *Twenty Hours,* a film, examined the 1956 uprising through one incident in a Hungarian village. The villian: a power-mad Communist party official who had gone berserk. One scene involved a fight between two friends, a dedicated Communist and a disenchanted individualist. "Who helped to educate your children?" the Communist demanded. "Did your son become a doctor—or a laborer of a lord like you were? . . . The count . . . employed your child when he was eight years old. . . He didn't build a house and school . . . he made things for his own pleasure. He had whores, places, a driver . . . Who took you out of misery and put you on your feet? . . . the workers' power." The embittered friend cried back: "And who else mocked me in my clearest sentiments, if not this power? . . . Who deceived me? Who told me that everything is mine, when nothing was mine? Who told me I was repeating the words of the enemy, when I wanted to tell the truth? Who . . . killed the innocents to ensure that nobody uttered a word, so no one dared to open their mouth, if not this power?"

In Budapest ten years after 1956, a playwright could dramatize his view that the System must never sacrifice or discard the individual; he could also mock the foibles of socialist bureaucracy. *The Iron Tooth of Time,* by Istvan

Csurka, concerned a bum who rolls drunks for a living. Seeking a more productive operation, he posed as a doctor and
informed officials that he would like to set up a clinic for
alcoholics. By Act III, he was in charge of a national chain
of clinics, represented Hungary on international commis-
sions, had been proposed for the Cabinet. And he was
miserable; he yearned for simpler days. In desperation, he
confessed to the police—who refused to believe him. Finally,
he sent a friend to report him to the government. "They
know all about you," the friend reported back, "but they
don't want to rock the boat."

Freedom was measured. A man might criticize the System; he might not challenge its existence. "There is no formal
censorship," an editor explained. "We give our material
directly to the printer. But everyone is responsible for what
he does. So we naturally conform with the basic policies and
directives."

Hungary remained a police state. The government retained the power, to use as it wished. When the public began
grumbling about price increases, plainclothes police boarded
streetcars, baited the passengers, then arrested those who
agreed loudest with their "complaints." The victims were
released with a warning, the arrests were publicized—the
point was made.

Their situation compelled Hungarians to practice that
pathetic logic to which people in tight situations are addicted.
"We have only one party, so we really don't need elections"
said one youngster seriously. An intellectual insisted that
free elections would be meaningless. "There is no opposition.
There are no personalities. How could I vote for them if I
don't know what they stand for? Free elections would do
nothing for this country at this time. Who would run?"

The logic of convenience was evident, too, in what little

discussion existed about 1956. Many viewed the uprising as a counterrevolution that had had to be suppressed after it was captured by extremist elements. All but forgotten were the democratic socialists who had been the intellectual force of the rebellion.

Freedom was further qualified by reality. As an editor observed, "Fifty-six taught us that we are going to build socialism—whatever that is—and we are going to be linked to the Soviet Union. Within this framework, many things have changed. The objectives of '56 have been realized—abolition of the dictatorship, freedom, material prosperity."

Socialist theory in Hungary ten years after the Revolution of 1956 was a mutation of Marxism and national character.

Hungarian character combines a reverence for what was with an irreverence for what is. Before the curtain rose at the Vidam Szinpad, a satiric theater, a player would step forward to "prove" how devoted the public had become to "democratic" life. "Tonight," he would say, "the audience will elect a master of ceremonies." Quickly, four "members of the audience" would propose a candidate—all four, the same man, a comedian named Alphonzo. Then the player would say: "All those who don't favor Alphonso can leave." No one would leave. Everyone would roar.

Pit humor against dialectic, and dialectic gives ground. Even party strategists acknowledged that national peculiarities were fragmenting once monolithic communism. "The period of conformity is over," a diplomat said, adding a caution worth pondering. "There are many ways to get to London. But the objective remains the same. In this sense, we may talk of eclecticism."

What was happening economically illustrated his point. Once, the planners thought that everything could be worked out more scientifically by central authorities. Now, they admitted that top-heavy socialism could not react in time to changing market factors. The two big words in Budapest by 1966 were "decentralize" and "motivate." Plant managers had authority to make crucial production decisions the moment the need for them became clear, rather than wait for the laborious official process to bring word to and from the top. And profit was soon to become a big factor in production. What the factory made above its quota, it would keep; what it kept, it might distribute in bonuses to the workers or invest in workers' vacation homes. Where the new economics had been tried, the effect had been electrifying. The manager of one pilot factory reported a fantastic increase in the efficiency and output of his workers. The first year, profits on some items rose 40 percent, his own earnings, 25 percent. Communist planners were admitting that they had discounted private motives too greatly.

Was this capitalism? "No," said an economist. "The U.S. is socializing its capitalism, but not adopting socialism. We are capitalizing socialism, but not abandoning socialism. Your means of production remain in private hands, ours in public. Let the market tell us what to produce, but it alone can't tell us how the country should develop."

"Up to now, we have said that profits are a capitalistic vestige," a party official said. "Now, we say that profits are useful for socialist purposes." He smiled when he said it.

In 1956, Hungarians were tearing themselves to shreds; ten years later, they were at peace. They had compromised, but their accomplishments remained remarkable. To a great extent, they had brought communism to terms with their own ideas. They had added fluidity to dogma. There was little question in their minds that materially they were better off. They wanted more freedom; they believed they would have it, once economic reforms had made life easier. Life was far from perfect, but it was better.

Which episode tells us the reality—Hungary or Czechoslovakia? When two such disparate symbols exist, a circle must be drawn large enough to include both.

One damp November day in 1968, I found myself in Zurich, en route to Bucharest, because three months earlier the Russians had gone to Prague. Zurich is to Europe's airplanes what Chicago once was to America's railroads. That day, headlines at the newspaper kiosk in the transit section of the terminal were speculating about a new Cold War. But Czech, Hungarian, and Rumanian planes were parked on the airfield, and inside the terminal, Czechs, Hungarians, and Rumanians milled freely with passengers from Western countries or stood in line to buy duty-free Scotch and cigarettes and perfumes.

Reality was neither the headlines nor the people alone, but the blend of both.

Twenty years ago, no Eastern European was in that airport or anywhere else outside the Iron Curtain unless he was on official business or under guard, and no Westerners were going East. Today, the number of weekly flights between Eastern and Western Europe approaches 1,000, the annual number of passengers, 2 million. A Pan American Airways subsidiary is finishing luxury hotels in Budapest, Bucharest, and Prague. Even Western credit cards are accepted currency in the East; more than 100 hotels and restaurants in Communist countries now honor the Diner's Club.

Twenty years ago, Russia awesomely ruled its world. Communist parties everywhere pledged primary allegiance to the USSR. Today, the monolith is fragmented, the Comintern is gone, the USSR is physically and emotionally threatened by another Communist power, Red China, which, in Russian minds, has replaced the United States as Enemy Number One.

Throughout the world, Communists are more Marxist nationalists than brothers in socialist revolt. Today, the unity of the left means infinitely more politically to Western Europe's Communists than does solidarity with the USSR. So, instinctively, they condemn the Czech invasion, for the simplest of reasons. To succeed as a political force, they need the issue of political freedom—because the workers in their countries fear loss of liberties if Communists were to take power. Much later, the Soviets manage to regain rhetorical support from party leaders by threatening to withdraw subsidies. But the heart is bared; the mind is known.

Twenty years ago, a cluster of eight Communist states buffered the Soviet Union. Today, Albania has split to China. Yugoslavia is the most vital socialist force within the neutral bloc. Rumania, predestined by Russian planning to be a raw-goods supplier for the USSR, has rejected its role, stalked from conferences, criticized the Russians, and established its own productive base. One year after the invasion of Czechoslovakia, a leading official of Rumania's Communist party laid it on the line to delegates at a party congress: "Where a cold abstract pattern, fettered, by narrow, unilateral tenets dominated our minds, live, ardent, stimulating thinking has made its way . . . Socialist humanism has walked out of the textbooks into our lives."

Twenty years ago, Russia could draw up master plans for the integration of Eastern European economies with her own in terms highly favorable to herself. In Moscow, in May, 1969, Hungarians, Poles, Bulgarians, Czechs, and East Germans were all willing to integrate—but each on different terms. And Rumania would not even discuss the matter.

Why this resistance arose could hardly be more simple, or more significant. Each country must make its own society work in terms of the needs of its peoples. The yield must be impressive or internal problems result.

The search for answers to these needs not only compels changes within, but leads each country to cast outward in search of assistance and trade. That trade leads to profound East-West contact that changes ideas and relationships. No man who has ever seen a cluster of young Rumanians bent over a British computer at a trade fair in Bucharest can forget the sight. East-West trade increases on the average 20 percent a year; Italy's efforts alone jumped almost 50 percent in one recent period.

The Cold War may not be over, but how very different it is from twenty years ago. Then Western Europe was prostrate, vulnerable to internal and external Communist threats. Today, Western Europe is healthy and impregnable, its six countries laced togeher by an economic structure, the Common Market, that not even France could escape—or would, if it could. Incidental to the union is a dividend greater by far than the capital gain. As a prelude to the *Common Market,* the six European countries were induced to partner coal and steel, the means of war. Because they did, a war provoked by Germany, which twice in twenty-five years took the world to arms, seems impossible.

That factor greatly affects Soviet calculations and dispositions. One indelible memory of prolonged contact with Russians is their enduring fear of the Germans. Whatever the fundamental reasons for the Russian intervention in Czechoslovakia, the diplomatic flirtation between that country and West Germany was certainly one of the factors.

The fear of Germany will never pass. But Russia's confidence in relation to it will grow. Today, that confidence is sufficient to permit a new nonaggression pact between West Germany and the USSR—which permits the Russians, in theory, at least, to focus their worries on China.

Russians are dogmatically paranoid. To any failure, they offer Stalin's answer: conspiracy. In the case of Czechoslovakia, that could have meant anything: a flight from socialism, a leap to the West. Their action was prompted by a mixture of small faith in man and a fear of invasion that dates back to the Tatars.

By their intrusion in Czechoslovakia, the Russians momentarily paralyzed the reform movement within the Socialist bloc. But they neither regained bloc solidarity nor destroyed the Communist progressives who press against the neo-Stalinists even in Russia itself.

Articles in the Soviet press confirm that the issues causing frictions between the Soviet Union and the more venturesome Socialist countries also produce frictions within the Kremlin. In 1968, there was division within the Kremlin over Czechoslovakia; today, there is division over the wisdom of economic reforms. Czechoslovakia dramatized the relationship between economic and political change; to conservatives like Leonid Brezhnev, such proof warranted a turn backward to economic centralism and revolutionary cheer leading. That is the point where the temptation is strongest to conclude that Russia will never change, that the moment reforms threaten control, party leaders strangle reforms. But if Russia is characterized by that truth today, it is equally characterized by the truth of 1965, when the leadership installed the reforms in the first place. Neither moment can be extracted from the historical process and made to stand, by itself, for the whole.

Even as the turn was being attempted, economist Alexander Birman, one of the guardians of the reforms, could issue public counsel whose equivalent was not to throw out the baby with the bath water; reforms were needed, he argued, and should not be jettisoned simply because they had been misapplied elsewhere. Society, he noted, does not abandon the use of money simply because some counterfeit bills appear.

Twenty-two years ago, a British writer named Eric Blair completed a novel that was to become the most important political metaphor of our times. Blair called himself George Orwell, and his book *Nineteen Eighty-Four.* It was the bitter testament of an idealist—he had fought in Spain for the Republicans—who had watched a humanistic ideal dehumanized by a vicious collective process. Blair's first use of this theme was in *Animal Farm,* the book that made him famous. Four years later, the theme had enlarged from allegory to a nightmare vision of the future. He set his tale in Oceania, one of three vast nations that together comprised the world. It was a world that had annihilated the individual; that terrorized rationality and impulse; that reached through hideous processes into the sacred regions of the soul to destroy each man's distinctive gifts. BIG BROTHER IS WATCHING YOU, said the caption on the poster that was everywhere, a poster of a man with a black moustache and probing eyes that seemed to follow your every move.

Orwell's target, of course, was totalitarianism, wherever it might arise, but no man alive could miss the specific analogy to Josef Stalin and the Soviet Union. There, the mentality for control and terror was already established; all that it lacked was the technological apparatus of *Nineteen Eighty-Four.* If Russia in 1949 did not have a telescreen that not only relentlessly broadcast propaganda but transmitted one's every sound and move, it nonetheless seemed to have inspired a madness not unlike that reflected in Oceania's slogans in 1984: "War is peace. Freedom is slavery. Ignorance is strength." Even without the Orwellian refinements, the Stalinists did not do badly. They killed millions, imprisoned scores of millions and spread their venom into Eastern Europe.

Orwell died in 1950. Twenty-one years later, we are only thirteen years from that symbolic date when individuality would have ceased to exist. How does the Russia of today compare to the Orwellian vision—which he, least of any man, would have wished confirmed?

The scores of thousands of political prisoners in the Soviet Union today are a condemnation of a political system by any democratic measure, but they are not equivalent to multimillions liquidated and even more millions imprisoned. It is important that these travesties be exposed and condemned; it is important that we maintain our bearings. Timed against her darkest hour, Russia has moved from midnight to dawn. If terror has not disappeared, it has at least shriveled. The threat of liquidation appears to have passed. Even assuming the present Soviet leadership wanted to, it could not, in all probability, crank up the liquidation apparatus. The conditions that permitted Stalin to mount it simply no longer exist.

Twenty years ago, Stalin ruled unassailably atop a machinery he had vitiated but secured by destroying 700,000 of his finest party members. The lesson of dissenters in Russia today is not simply that they suffer, but also that they can signal their dissent in ways they could not before.

In the diary of his ordeal in a Soviet asylum, General Pyotr Grigorenko recounts how he reminded a commission called to assess his sanity of how drastically the fact of protest has changed in the Soviet Union. Under Stalin, he pointed out, dissenters formed secret Lenin organizations, published illegal tracts, called for a new revolution. "Today there are no more secret organizations and no more tracts, but instead public and courageous declarations against flagrant abuses, against lies and hypocrisy. Today, there is a fight for the rigorous respect of the laws and the constitutional rights of the people. Today it is a public battle, within the law, for the democratization of our society."

Russia is not monolithic. Opposition does exist, and change, therefore, does have a chance. But it is imperative that we recognize the character of this opposition, rather than distort reality with our wish. It is loyal opposition that exists. It is the perfecting of socialism that is at issue, not its overthrow.

Change, if it comes, will come not because of a revolt, but because of Russia's need to perform. For the country to do that, the leaders must eventually pay attention to the progressives who counsel change.

What all the trends and episodes taken together tell us is that the framework that encompasses the socialist world will remain what it is. But within that framework, a degree of change remains possible—and can still occur.

Will it? A "yes" or a "no" answer would be equally absurd. Only an estimate is possible. Here is Ota Sik's, eighteen months after his ouster, speaking from his professor's chair in Basel:

"The ideological obstacles are very strong, always returning the economy to the strongest centralization. And so you have a very clear contradiction between the needs of the economy and political and ideological hindrances. What will win? It is difficult to say. For the time being . . . the political pressures are greater. But in the long run, without liberalization and use of market functions, the socialist economy cannot win. So over the long run, I think our ideas will come through."

CHAPTER EIGHT

1985

Why one generation acts one way and another, another way is due, in large part, to the condition of the world at the time each comes of age. One reason today's younger generation reacts with such puzzlement and even scorn toward the Cold War is surely because that war has changed so profoundly in the quarter century since it began.

It might profit the younger generation, as well as lift the quality of dialogue a notch, if it were to make the "imaginative leap" into its parents' shoes, and ask what its own reaction might have been had it been assailed by the same set of facts.

The causation of facts can be the subject of argument. But the facts themselves cannot.

It is a fact that Marxism and Leninism both presupposed a gravitation toward socialism by all the countries of the world.

It is a fact that in the volumes of Lenin's writings, predictions of Russian-inspired revolutions in capitalist countries (which, to Lenin, had no legitimate reason to exist) appear as prominently as theories of peaceful coexistence.

It is fact that the Soviet socialist state fashioned by Lenin and secured by Stalin provided these capitalist countries with a chilling vision of their fate should the Marxist-Leninist predictions come true.

It is a fact that wherever Russia assisted Communists to take power, the opening acts against the freedom of man were played exactly to script: tortures, false confessions, show trials, summary executions, and the forced submission of millions.

These are the facts on which a generation was raised, and no amount of juggling can erase them from the ledger. Any extreme threat produces an extreme reaction to it; in the threat posed by Stalin's inhumanity and the system he fashioned to spread it lies the cause of America's rearmament —and eventual reactionary excesses.

Where history can serve us further is in demonstrating how these appalling and threatening facts have slowly evolved to the reality we know today:

How, in defiance of all theoretical predictions, the capitalist states not only survived the "inherent" contradictions that would assertedly spell their doom, but turned increasingly to public power and liberal economic reforms to negate their systems' abuses.

How, as a consequence, the world revolution anticipated by the Marxist-Leninists developed into a standoff between communism and capitalism, another defiance of historical projection.

How an exterior menace united the rivals in an effort to save one another, thereby confusing, if not destroying, the issue of capitalistic "legitimacy" for the peoples of the socialist bloc.

How atomic power raised the price of direct, overt confrontation to an unsupportable cost.

How all of these factors combined to alter Russia's view of the U.S. and other democratic powers as well as its strategy for preeminence, and give the country the perspective it offers to a new generation today.

Twenty years ago, Stalin used political conquest to create a fortress of land around Russia and "prevent," thereby, its "encirclement" by capitalist countries. Today, Russia's leaders find a certain comfort in *de facto* coexistence. "Fifteen years ago, the Cold War was at its peak," André Fontaine, author of *History of the Cold War,* observed in *Le Monde,* in May, 1969:

. . . Today, coexistence has replaced the Cold War. It may not be peace—that would suppose a heartfelt reconciliation—but it is at least an armistice. Its basis is the division of the world into two spheres of influence, and neither Washington nor Moscow believes that it has the power to alter this balance in the near future. Hence feelings of apprehension have diminished, indeed very nearly disappeared. . . .

"No one, in fact," he noted a few months later, "aside from diplomatic and military circles and a few rightist politicians, believes now in the reality of a Soviet threat."

When we assess what remains of communism, we see that the Russians have abandoned the original Leninist quest for world revolution by force, in exchange for other, more subtle techniques. War between the great powers is impermissible, but wars of national liberation are fine. Confrontation is out, but competition is in, particularly for influence among the nations of the Third World. The richest irony, perhaps, is that Russia now stands watch against Lenin's True Believers and revolutionary custodians, the Chinese.

In the meanwhile, the forces favoring polycentrism are glacially transforming most of the Communist world.

Had the conditions existing today been a part of the Cold War generation's reality, that generation might well have reacted differently than it did. Because those conditions

pertain today does not mean that the Cold War generation
will see the same image in the prism that others profess to
see. The memory of its earlier shape will always distort, to
some extent, the appearance of current reality.

What might lift the quality of dialogue yet another
notch would be a corollary effort by the Cold War generation
to visualize what reality looks like today to those whose perceptions are *not* affected so powerfully by anterior facts. What
these people perceive is a drama that has played past its
ending. This is how it goes:

In the process of pursuing the American Obsession, we
have polluted the American Dream. In so doing, we have
imperiled the very victory our military expenditures were
meant to assure, and destroyed what we meant to protect.

In the eyes of the world, our response has become more
evil than the evil now opposed. Whatever we have "gained"
in militarily neutralized territories, we have lost in the contempt we arouse for our methods and the suspicions of our
intent. To much of the rest of the world, we have the posture
of imperialists, acting as imperialist powers have historically
acted to preserve the status quo. In this endeavor, we have,
on occasion, enlisted the Mafia of international affairs.

But the danger to our posture is not so much from the
lack of solid ground beneath our international commitment
as it is from the erosion of our own soil at home.

The most dangerous threat to the United States today is
not military domination by a foreign power. It is the loss of
faith by peoples everywhere, including the United States, in
what America can mean.

What savage irony it is (the drama continues) that more
and more, in freedom's name, we invoke Orwellian processes.
If our government spends more than 70 cents of every budget
dollar on past, present, and future wars, as Richard J. Barnet

documents in *The Economy of Death,* is that not some indication of a conviction by some of us that "war is peace?" If some of us sanction censorship and intimidation of the press, believe that dissent must be crushed, and become impatient with due process; if we arrange preventive detention and police right-of-entry laws and continue to sanction wiretapping; if our federal government lies to the people as an act of deliberate policy and spends millions of dollars of tax money to write its own version of history, does that not suggest a fear of freedom so paralyzing that totalitarianism can result?

No objective American would acknowledge that this Orwellian development is consistent with the American tradition; nor would he permit it to stand as a description of that tradition. Nonetheless, its resemblance to even a portion of the American reality shows how far we have strayed from our aims.

The most compelling reason why Marxism remains a persistent vision is that our own has not matured.

For years, we have indulged ourselves with the belief that the rest of the world wanted nothing so much as to duplicate the American way of life—as though the guarantee of food, shelter, education, leisure, joy was somehow an American invention.

People everywhere are enthralled by the American capacity to achieve. They are appalled by our capacity for neglect.

Much of the world views us with emotions ranging from perplexity to pity to horror. It does not comprehend how we can even consider funds for an airplane that will cross the ocean in $2\frac{1}{2}$ hours while we deny funds for a program to exterminate rats in the ghettos. The "answer" is that we must build and sell supersonic aircraft to protect our balance of payments. Critics reply that when our balance of payments takes precedence over the balance of life, something is wrong with our balance of values.

There is only one way we can validate the American Obsession to save the world for Democracy, according to this script. We must make Democracy work at home. We must diminish the American Obsession so that we may resurrect the American Dream. What we would lose by not supporting militarily many a feeble political anachronism would probably be lost eventually. What we would gain would be a country that again believed in itself. Such an achievement, paradoxically, would win us more "ground" than any kind of force.

What might conceivably happen if we were to revise the drama?

George Orwell's metaphor of freedom's death is not the least invalid. But the likelihood that it might be transformed to fact is perhaps sufficiently diminished to make an alternative projection possible. We can at least begin to ponder what might lie beyond 1984, that wishful time when words would have achieved approximately the same meanings for peoples in different worlds.

The process of biological evolution is a near-perfect metaphor of political growth. As the function of a political organ changes, so does its form. If the change makes the political organism a little better and more efficient, then, just like any biological strain, the political organism establishes a standard with which other, less talented systems cannot compete. Only here does the comparison turn gently from course. In time, those systems less fit to survive tend not to disappear, as do biological species, but to assume secondary roles in world affairs as smaller components of a larger whole (the city-state) or vestigial elements of the system (monarchy).

Today, each of our two major political systems is well into the process of evolutionary change. As with biological evolution, the process is powered by the need to survive. What is most striking about both the cause and effect of the phenomenon is the symmetry exposed when the elements are joined.

Both systems are losing, not winning, their battles for ideological influence with the rest of the world. If we sometimes have the sensation that the Russians are gaining at our expense, it is only because there are moments when we are losing credibility at a faster rate than they are.

Neither system has achieved the political goal it seeks above all others—the establishment of a model that others find alluring.

Suppose you were a young economist of an underdeveloped country shopping for an effective social system. Your criteria would be both theoretical and technical, but your fundamental question would be simple and historical: Which system best develops and utilizes the individual so that he may freely realize his greatest potential while at the same time contributing to the common good? Your answer, most likely, would be neither.

You would not fail to see that central planning, Soviet style, is the mother of twins—inefficiency and repression. You would not wish to impose on your people a system like that imposed on Eastern Europe after World War II. You would not aspire, any more than Eastern European countries aspire, to the juiceless conformity of the Soviet life style.

By contrast, you could hardly accept as a model a system one-fifth of whose people live below the minimum subsistence level; that pays some citizens not to produce food while other citizens go hungry; that appears to require a permanent population of several million unemployed persons to assure wage and price stability; that periodically imposes deflationary measures which weigh most heavily on those who can least support them. You would know that the United States has the highest rate of violence of all the modern, stable nations; you would learn that, for all its racial overtones, violence in the world's richest nation is primarily caused by poverty. Faced with the possibility of a revolutionary situation in your underdeveloped country, you would remark the existence of revolutionary pockets in the most highly developed nation on earth.

At this point, you might sit down and draw up a shopping list of individual items that you might like to buy separately from each store. From the communist store, you might list the power to marshal a country's resources for the purpose of rapid brute development. You might also list the system of egalitarian social care. From the capitalist store you would surely list the creativity, the efficiency, the power of private enterprise. You would certainly list the potential for maximum personal liberty and growth. Then you might sigh and consider how much simpler your task would be if the items you had listed were all included in one store.

It might be somewhat comforting to learn that others were already at work on the same kind of list. It goes under the heading "convergence."

The word has been used by others, but it was Andrei D. Sakharov, the father of the Soviet H-bomb and one of Russia's most courageous and emancipated intellectuals, who gave the idea shape. Sakharov, in a 1968 declaration, suggested that the Soviet and American systems were drawing together, and that one day, through a series of modifications of their respective institutions, the gap between them would be so slight that cooperation would be assured.

The idea is repugnant to orthodox thinkers—both doctrinaire Marxists and inveterate anti-Communists—and some of Sakharov's extensions are admittedly sheer fancy. But there are compelling reasons—symmetrical reasons—why the process is neither so wishful nor so impossible as it seems.

It is within each system itself that this symmetry is most strikingly exposed.

Each sees that its military spends too much and has to be curtailed. Each finds curtailment resisted by military-industrial complexes spoiled by a quarter century of lavish care. Each must break the cycle of military escalation or be buried in the environmental refuse endemic to any highly industrialized society, regardless of political philosophy. Each is beholden to the companion of success, the rising expectations of its peoples.

Both systems have pliant, patriotic masses that for psychological reasons have historically tended to accept the reality they inherit. What is new and different from even twenty years ago is that each system today also includes an intelligent, restless minority insisting that the system has veered wildly from course.

What follows cannot be proved. And yet it is not pure conjecture. Perhaps the best description is projection launched from a platform of ideas. It is an effort to synthesize the viewpoints of reformers in both East and West. Taken together, their viewpoints tell us what life might conceivably be like in the symbolic year 1985.

These intelligent, restless minorities, these men who flavor the age, appear to be converging on certain telling insights about the realities of each system.

There is a maturing suspicion among some of its greatest beneficiaries that capitalism may never be able to provide for all members of its society in acceptable fashion until and unless it is regulated to a much greater degree than today.

There is a maturing suspicion among Marxists, who staunchly maintain their vision, that communism may never be able to provide for all members of its society in acceptable fashion until and unless it provides room for individual will and choice.

The men to whom the above descriptions apply are converging on certain values:

That the individual must not be lost within any social framework.

That the social framework, by contrast, must be sufficiently large to encompass all.

Convergence, then, would be an attempt to reconcile individualism and order, not order at the price of individualism, not individualism at the price of order, but an orchestration that maximizes individualism in the most harmonious possible order.

How you eventually did that would depend on where you were politically and historically. There is no single answer, or truth, to be applied in all cases. That knowledge, itself, is a unifying truth. There are others.

It is perfectly evident that totalitarian solutions, attempted in whatever name, will exercise the latent tendency in man for power, destroy his originality, and create its own hell on earth.

It is perfectly evident that uncontrolled government, with no true opposition, will adhere dogmatically to the ideas that projected it to power—not always for the venal reasons ascribed, but simply in the rationalized conviction that its original thoughts were true.

It is perfectly evident, at the other extreme, that a

democratic society does not function properly where the government does not, with vigor and law, enforce the national priorities—priorities about which there should be no conceivable argument. Who is for pollution or poverty or the uncontrolled expansion of our military arsenal beyond any imaginable need? Yet our own experience tells us that men who learn how to use government can seduce it into believing that by serving them it is serving the public good.

The conservative is right when he hallows individualism. He is wrong when, in its name, he inflicts injury on others.

The socialist is right when he plumps for public power to create the social action private power has failed to produce. He is wrong when he squeezes the juice from life.

The Marxists find it abhorrent that we would permit our lives to be governed by something so intrinsically vicious as the marketplace, wherein only the fittest survive. But they have learned that without the stirring effects of competition, even highly motivated men become stale, sluggish, careless, disinterested.

We have learned that competition can tune an engine until its parts mesh and its power reaches maximum efficient levels. But we have found that competition so annihilates both the weakest within our society and the companion aspects of the self that we are beset by problems, guilts, and anxieties that make life burdensome and shallow.

Convergence blends these discoveries.

Perhaps man is, as many behaviorists contend, inherently aggressive and selfish. But this does not prove that man is inherently stupid. Confronted with need, he adjusts. It is this adjustment that the reformers are urging today.

Socialism's reformers are the cutting edge to more personal liberty.

Our reformers are the cutting edge toward more social justice.

Each is attempting to cut toward the ample center where the two cultures could meet.

Should they ever meet, it would be as half apple and half orange, not as two halves of one fruit.

The one fundamental distinction between the systems is irresoluble, permanent, unbridgeable—the ownership of property. Whatever forms of regulation our own society eventually applies to private enterprise, ownership of this enterprise will remain in private hands. Whatever forms of incentive socialism eventually employs, be it profit-sharing, free-market economies, or local control, the people will retain ownership of the means of production.

This is not an imposed idea; rather, it is one broadly shared throughout the socialist system. I cannot forget the response of a Czech writer who had been an unrelenting critic of the Novotny regime and an instrument of Czechoslovakia's golden spring. During a long dinner one night in Prague, he listed for me all the errors and problems and hardships that had been associated with the first twenty years of socialism. When he finished I asked him, "Do you accept the socialist premise?" He answered at once, "Absolutely."

I remember the words of my friend Nicolai Amosoff, a cybernetics wizard, a deputy of the Supreme Soviet, the best-known doctor in the Soviet Union, whose fictionalized journal of two days in a surgeon's life, *The Open Heart,* has been read by millions of Russians in book and serial form:

"We understand that capitalism is evolving into higher forms; we no longer hold the primitive view that it is predatory. But the thirst for power is part of human nature, an extension of the instinct to hurt. Private property is a stimulant to the instinct for power. A rational society is not possible without a drastic limitation of private property."

It is par for the course to dismiss someone else's action as further proof of the enduring wisdom of Machiavelli. What ought to be acknowledged, and isn't, is that some of an opponent's action might arise from conviction. To an extent, the doctrinaire socialist may fear the price mechanism because it embodies freedoms that might threaten his power structure. He may also fear the price mechanism because he truly believes that the social inequities of capitalism are inevitable distortions of a system based on the power to buy and sell.

But the vision of the Marxists is clearing. "Two or three years ago, our students developed the suspicion that the way in which Marx was being presented was false," a Czech professor told me in the spring of 1968. "The interpretations of Marx that came from the West didn't coincide with the interpretations of the Russians. The Russians left out certain things—statements regarding freedom of speech, of gathering, statements that were not hostile enough to the system the Russians were against.

"Marx never spoke of a human being like human material. One is an individual who is not determined from outside but from inside, not an object, but a subject with his own personality who can form himself and change himself. In this point of view the Russians don't stick to Marx. This is the difference between the theory of Marx and this so-called Marxist ideology."

The enduring lesson of Czechoslovakia is not that it failed but that it happened—a revelation of what the Communists had learned about the nature of man and the kind of society that ought to be organized around him, a socialist society to be sure, but humane, man-oriented, and free.

The Czech's golden spring of 1968 may yet prove to be a moment in time on which history will pivot. What that time exposed was how far the socialists had moved in the direction of democratic values. I recall an exchange with Eduard Goldstuecker, a lifelong Communist, vice-rector of Charles University, president of the Czech writer's union, and a leader of the writers' rebellion that early in 1968 helped tumble the party conservatives. In the light of events, his comment is ironic. But it shows how closely the edge of socialist thought has cut toward our own.

"What is socialist democracy?" I asked. "When we speak of democracy do we mean the same thing?"

"I think we mean basically the same thing by democracy: a system in which the fundamental rights and liberties of the citizen are guaranteed by law."

"Could we catalogue these fundamental rights?"

"Certainly. They are catalogued in your constitution and will be catalogued in our constitution soon."

In that remark, perhaps, lies the reason why almost a quarter century after the Cold War began, the United States found itself wishing mightily for the success of a Communist regime.

What we are converging on, then, is not a system. It is a state of mind.

We are each saying that man should not be a cipher at the mercy of amorphous forms.

We know now where this voyage could conceivably take the Marxists. Where could it take us?

The quality of life in America today reflects a historic ambivalence toward power. We have been so frightened of amorphous power that we have used power inadequately in both places where power is required. We have had neither the central power to express our vision of society as it ought to be nor the local power to realize this vision with concrete acts.

We now know what kind of life this ambivalence has produced. It is a life in which growth for its own sake has vitiated our land; in which 5 million people over the age of sixty-five are classified by our government as "poor;" in which young, well-educated, well-inclined parents cannot live in cities because their children cannot be educated in public schools. For our affluence, we receive air that is unbreathable and water in which we cannot swim and fish cannot live. We can scarcely ride our railroads. We joke about the Long Island Expressway—"the longest parking lot in the world"— but five days a week, 300 days a year that joke is reality for hundreds of thousands of Americans, breathing poisonous fumes, manufacturing bile that attacks their inner linings and subtracts days or months or years from lives already impoverished by wasted time.

How have we managed to inflict these punishments on ourselves? Basically, we are getting the life we are buying. We Americans, with the highest per capita income in the world, spend only 28.2 percent of our gross national product on the national welfare. The Swedes, with the second highest income, spend 41 percent.

Historically we have so favored private spending over public spending that today even protection against crime has become a matter of private enforcement. Because society has failed to supply the public monies required to attack crime at its source and sufficiently protect individuals, individuals have now begun to buy their own protection. An image of what such a tendency might produce has been conjured by the National Commission on the Causes and Prevention of Violence. It is an image of central-city business districts deserted at night, except for armed patrols; of high-rise fortresses in choice city locations; of "sanitized corridors" connecting safe living areas; of armored homes and cars and armed guards riding shotgun on all public transportation.

Should that dark vision materialize, it will be the ultimate proof of what poor buys bargains can be.

We have neither the central power to marshal a fight against the causes of crime, nor the local power to fight crime itself. We have neither because we refuse to provide them. We refuse because we fear their political and fiscal implications. The first means more government. The second means more taxes.

Crime derives from national causes, not local ones. Poverty is not a local issue. Migration is not a local issue. Addiction is not a local issue. It is not for New York and Chicago and Los Angeles and Detroit to suffer the burdens caused by society's failure to achieve social justice for rural blacks who migrate to cities in despair.

For years we have lived with a welfare system that satisfies no one—not the recipient degraded by its processes, not the taxpayer resentful of his burden. We pay a great deal and see little result; poverty may diminish statistically, but neither its mood nor appearance seem to change.

The negative income tax reflects a more emancipated view of our society's responsibility than has ever existed before. But it is actually founded on a conservative approach to welfare aimed at avoiding the welfare state. Its objective is to provide for the unfortunate among us while at the same time preserving independence of choice.

The idea could work, but nothing suggests that it will. On the contrary, most evidence around us suggests that we have little to show for our welfare precisely because it is poorly applied. Without well-organized services dispensing specific assistance, there is simply no way to assure that welfare benefits matter.

We are properly horrified by the boondoggling, inefficiency and lack of imagination that unfortunately characterize much American bureaucracy. But if we have inherited such conditions, it is because of the contempt in which we have historically held government and its functions. We both underpay and disrespect many of our career service people. Once again, we are getting what we're buying.

We expect, more than any other people, that our private enterprise will produce efficient and profitable results. We expect our public enterprise to be slothful, inefficient, and, in all probability, corrupt. Our expectations precisely reflect an overbalanced value on individual versus social action. One result is that, unlike any other major country, our government, which is, after all, the industry that affects us most, does not attract our best people. Is it any wonder, then, that after all these years of less-than-the-best effort directed to the running of the country, we find ourselves needing to create presidential committees on the national priorities?

Until very recently any suggestions that our national priorities be planned were met with cries of "socialism."

Today we are beginning to realize that we need central power with real power—not simply the power to legislate, but to monitor its acts and then reform them if they do not work out as expected. But at the same time we must have more effective application and control of that power in the form of local executors. One is vision, the other muscle.

What happens when central power sufficiently expresses the national will and local power firmly implements that will? *Is* there a system in which society's vision is amply expressed at the central level and then so concretized at the local level that each citizen feels he benefits? Most observers of the social order would agree that if anyone has come close, it's Sweden. They would also contend that if we want to see where we're heading, Sweden's the place to look.

It's often argued that Sweden, with a small, homogeneous society and no racial problem, has little relevance for us. The argument begs the point. Italy has no color problem, and its people are essentially homogeneous. They are also at one another's throats. Ultimately, the problem of social harmony is not one of color, but need. It bears repeating that a man whose needs are well provided for will make a better neighbor than a man whose needs are not.

Sweden's central vision is that the state must guarantee those provisions because they will not otherwise materialize.

"The old conservative vision was that with four per cent growth a year you will have twice as much national income in 25 years," Prime Minister Olof Palme explained during a long talk we had in Stockholm. "In that case, it's ridiculous to talk about distribution because everybody will be so much happier when there's twice as much income and the problems of distribution will automatically solve themselves. I think that was said 100 years ago and I think that experience shows that automatic market forces work in exactly the opposite direction—towards increasing gaps between people."

Sweden has her problems: Rising crime and violence. Restless kids. A housing shortage. Alienation, particularly among people in the green-belt apartment clusters that ring the cities. But strung together, these troubles are as misleading as the country's infamous suicide rate, which suffers from an honest count that doesn't exist where law or religion condemn the act; which is not the world's highest by far; and which has increased only slightly since the turn of the century.

Social critics see the problems as inevitable consequences of urbanizing a traditionally rural culture and as short-term dislocations within a long-range program that the people want. If in Sweden there is absence of social drama, as many rightly complain, it is because there is absence of social suffering. Where our urban chaos today threatens the national will, beneath Sweden's headlines lies a serene conviction that her priorities are in order.

The people who administer those priorities, the Social Democrats, have retained political primacy for more than thirty years, which makes the exposés of foreign journalists about frustrated, unhappy Swedes so much wish-projection, what Gunnar Myrdal calls "compensating rationalization of envy." As Myrdal wrote recently, in the *New York Times:*

"If there is continually full employment, so that mass unemployment is disappearing from the horizon; if there is an increasingly effective public service for aiding those individuals in danger of becoming unemployed in a lagging industry, so that even the exceptional unemployment risk is reduced; if all citizens in case of illness have at their disposal medical facilities for only a nominal fee; if they can look forward to a pension in old age that, in stable value, will amount to two-thirds of their income on their best fifteen years; if decent living standards are guaranteed by the state for children, widows, invalids, and handicapped; if by law it is forbidden to dismiss a woman for family reasons; if women in public service before and after childbirth are given paid leave from employment and all women are compensated for various costs relating to the event; if all schools are free and the students and their families also are gradually relieved from the necessity of finding support for their living costs; if strenuous efforts are made to help families in modest circumstances to get a decent home to live in; and so on—how can that make people feel unhappy and less free and relaxed?"

On the contrary, the happiest, most free and relaxed people I have ever met are two attractive young Swedes.

Runo and Cay Edström live in Stockholm. Runo produces television programs. Cay markets literary properties. What they keep of what they earn would make most Americans shudder. Yet, they seem perennially to glow. There are obvious reasons why. They are in love. They enjoy their work. And they've recently bought a house to shelter a growing brood. But a good percentage of their contentment is profit from an asset we Americans have suddenly found missing from the vault—a sound, secure, environment. With just $8,ooo to spend a year—half of what they earn—Runo and Cay live well in a livable town.

Why their town is livable, and what it does to them, offer some pertinent lessons for us.

In Sweden, the city comes first. City fathers have powers unrealized in the U.S. In the city's name, they buy up its land. No developer with a flashy scale model and seductive figures turns a zoning board's head. The city's well-paid planners, fortified by outside counsel and public debate, determine what's best for the city as well as for the private builder. They then invite the builder to build.

But it's the city's power to tax that really boggles an American mind. Each municipality has an unlimited right to charge what it requires to meet projected expenses. The city fathers simply add up the amounts needed to run and develop their city. From this total, they subtract the national government's contribution to the city—25 percent on the average. Then they subtract their city's income taxes on local industry and their revenue from city-owned apartments. The remainder must be covered by the residents. Last year,

Stockholm took 19 percent of its residents' taxable income, slightly under the national average. (In the U.S., city income taxes seldom exceed one percent.)

The Swedes know that's what it takes, and that is that. If the city needs more the next year, it takes more the next year, and that continues to be that.

What does this mean for the Edströms?

Runo earns $700 a month as a producer-director for the Swedish Broadcasting Corporation. Cay earns $400 from her literary agency. Free-lance television assignments for Runo and modeling jobs for Cay can push their annual income to $16,000.

They pay about $4,000 in national taxes. They pay $2,750 to their city government. Another $1,250 in estimated indirect taxes pushes their total tax bill to $8,000 a year.

It's the second figure that concerns us here. Of all the taxes the Edströms pay, one-third goes to the administrative unit most directly affecting their lives—their city.

A New Yorker earning $16,000 a year would pay total taxes just under $4,000, half what the Edströms pay. If he owned his home, as the Edströms do, he would contribute $1,150 of that amount to his city, mostly in property taxes— a tax lightly used in Sweden. Even though national-government support to cities, such as exists in Sweden, is unknown in the United States, what the New Yorker pays for his city is well less than half what the Edströms pay in Stockholm. And compared to other U.S. city residents, New Yorkers pay a lot.

So the Edströms, like other Swedes, are paying more for their cities than we are. Are they getting more by paying more? Would we?

Some of the answers can be expressed in amounts projected by Swedish finance officials. The figures are estimates

of what a family like the Edströms gets back for what it gives
in taxes. For example, the Edströms' four-year-old daughter
Mikki goes to nursery, thus enabling Cay to work. The Edströms pay $4 for Mikki's full-day program, including a meal
—which covers about half the $2,200-a-year cost. The city
pays $640; the national government pays the rest.

In February, 1970, Cay had her second baby, a boy. Her
only charge was the $30 extra she paid to enjoy a private
room for a week. So in 1970, the Edströms received more
than their share of the $230 hospital subsidy projected for a
family like them.

When the Edström children go to school, each child will
receive support worth $520 a year.

Such "visible" items, as Stockholm's budget office describes them, would bring the Edströms' benefits to about
$1,500, if they were fully used. But, much of what the Ed-
ströms get for their money isn't "visible" at all.

About $60 of what the Edströms pay their city is set aside
to help support its transportation system, should fares not
cover costs. The Edströms' return on that is intangible—the
use, when they need it, of a system that works. From their
home in an outlying district of Stockholm, a bus-and-subway
combination takes them to the city center in 25 minutes.
It's 28 cents for a fast, clean ride.

Even so seemingly simple an issue as transportation raises
a critical point. If some of the Edströms' benefits are not
visible, neither are some of our taxes.

Each time we take a taxi or drive to work not because
we prefer to but because our transit systems aren't good, we
are paying a hidden tax. Each time we pay a private-school
bill because public schools are inadequate, we are paying a
hidden tax. Each time we pay inflated prices for food because
clogged streets increase delivery costs, we are paying a hidden

tax. Perhaps the blackest joke of all is on the man who buys protection. He, too, is paying a hidden tax.

As our society continues to deteriorate, our hidden taxes increase—much as do the costs of maintaining an outworn car. The irony of our tax-avoidance policy is how very expensive it is.

Another invisible benefit: 18 percent of the Edströms' local tax—about $500—goes to what Stockholm's budget office describes as the "increase of public fortune." The most obvious use of this money is for land purchases the Edströms might not "see," but that ensure their city's character and future.

Seldom have our cities done the same. Their development has been a largely haphazard affair—the most constant ingredient, a developer understandably interested in profit. The developer gathers parcels of land, and offers a plan to exploit them. The city may ask for some changes, but seldom refuses the project.

That system has now come under attack from the highest possible source. In his State of the Union message on January 22, 1970, President Nixon declared: "As our cities and suburbs relentlessly expand, those priceless open spaces needed for recreation areas accessible to their people are swallowed up, often forever. Unless we preserve these spaces while they are still available, we will have none to preserve. Therefore, I shall propose new financing methods for purchasing open space and parklands now, before they are lost to us."

It is just one step from President Nixon's proposal to Stockholm's program of buying land surrounding the city before it is developed—so that its constructive development is assured. Already, two Colorado communities, Boulder and Aspen, have approved sales taxes to finance the purchase of surrounding lands. How long we have taken to learn; how needlessly our cities have been ruined!

A small part of the Edströms' taxes finances studies that determine how their city should grow. Private enterprise can then build for a profit—to the specification of expert plans.

Our taxes theoretically pay for that too. But there's a difference. Most U.S. cities haven't the money to offer attractive wages to planners, so the best ones don't always work for the cities. Stockholm and other Swedish cities offer competitive wages to planners—the best ones do work for them.

Because the city has the means, it can take the offensive in determining how it will grow. It wastes little, if any, time on the preoccupying concerns of our city planners—undoing damage already done, or trying to prevent its spread.

Our city planners advise and forecast, but they do not usually command. Stockholm, like most European cities, has the power to carry out a thoroughly thought-out master plan. Part of this power is political, but part is surely the financial means to execute the planners' ideas.

Perhaps the most critical item on the Edströms' tax list is so invisible it does not even appear in the Budget Director's records. It is part of the extra share the Edströms put into the kitty—an investment in better neighbors.

In addition to paying to send Mikki to nursery each day, the Edströms pay taxes that help send the child of lower-than-average wage earners to nursery at no cost to them. They know precisely what they're doing, and they don't mind a bit.

If you play the game with visible items, the Edströms come out losers. But they don't view it that way.

Somehow, in high-priced Stockholm, the Edströms manage dinner out once a fortnight, and save enough for a vacation. They make do with $640 a month, and they wind up the year without money. But they bear absolutely no grudge about taxes. "It gives me safety," says Runo. "It's absolutely worth it. I know that Mikki can go to the nursery. I know I have my job security. I know I'll be taken care of if I'm ill."

This is the heart of the matter. If Runo and Cay are content it is because they are getting their money's worth for the taxes they pay their city. They receive tangible benefits for their money. They receive intangible benefits, as well. They live in a city that is organized to deal with its problems, and whose residents give it the means. Their contribution is founded on broad national policy, which contends that taxation is the only means of reducing social inequities in a society that wants to be free.

One of the major arguments against the welfare state is that it would curb initiative. Some private capital has fled the country, and some young Swedes are emigrating, or plan to. But if restrictions on upper earning limits have cramped the competitive urge, there is little evidence of it in Sweden.

"We have a new competitive part of life much more cruel than the old one," says a welfare official. "Formerly, only those who could afford it could get an education. Today, anyone in our society can compete. The only thing that can keep a man from being anything he wants is his brains."

Recent studies indicate that the urge to advance is as strong as it is in the U.S. Businessmen compete with one another for jobs carrying all-important fringe benefits. Between 10 and 20 percent of Swedes, it is estimated, take extra jobs. Nor is there any indication at the lower earning levels that too many benefits will make people stop working. "We work for the love of work," Gunnar Myrdal insists. An experience of Dr. Lennart Levi of the Karolinska Institutet, a specialist on stress, bears him out. Of 139 physically and socially handicapped Swedes he helped rehabilitate, 138 returned to work; only one elected to coast on his social welfare benefits.

"Social security is not a reasonable alternative to work," says a welfare official. "It's followed by a definite fall in living standards. This is not accidental."

"I don't think Swedes are working any less because of the taxes. We can't find any proof of that," says a spokesman for the Swedish Taxpayers Association, which watchdogs expenditures and fights those it feels will curtail growth. "Of course people don't like taxes. No one does. But where you put it to a point where they choose more expenditures or lower taxes, people choose expenditures. Political parties have tried to get votes with lower taxes, but they haven't succeeded. Now no political party in Sweden is trying hard to succeed politically with lower taxes."

Sweden's solutions are not perfect. The country has yet to devise formulas that keep some taxpayers from cheating. Nor do all taxpayers obtain the benefits available. But many of its features are worth considering. One is the national government's concept of its responsibility to the city. Where problems are of national origin, like crime, is not the national government obliged to furnish cities the means to cure their woes? Sweden's answer is yes —it supports its cities directly, for example, by payment of policemen's salaries. Its support is indirect, as well, in the consideration it gives each taxpayer for the taxes he pays to his city.

But what is most vital is the sense of value, of *participation,* each taxpayer receives for his contribution.

Sweden's defense establishment takes 14 percent of its national budget. Our own takes 36 percent. Should our priorities ever be reordered, and our cities put first, the federal government need not necessarily make a direct contribution. The same effect could be achieved indirectly if cities sharply raised residents' income taxes and the government generously discounted such taxes. With as much money at stake in our cities as the Edströms have in theirs, Americans would be highly motivated to be sure they'd get a return.

Most of the rich Western nations have drawn closer and closer in recent years to the Swedish model. Our own is no exception. Our path toward convergence lies through a democratic and capitalistic welfare state that profits from the creative power of private enterprise, directs this power into socially constructive channels, and protects its weakest members from the hardships and shame of exclusion.

That the United States is well along this road can be bemoaned, but it can scarcely longer be argued. If there was ever any doubt, our social legislation of the 1960s has erased it. More important than the legislation itself is the new attitude toward power it expresses.

It is amorphous power that is so horrifying, because it is so anonymous. That doesn't disqualify power. We need enabling power to achieve broad objectives, and specific power applied to specific wrongs—in our communities, our universities, our local schools. What we don't need is amorphous power that denies a man his being.

That is a discovery we share with most of the rest of the world. That is the discovery—the convergent discovery—causing all the clamor.

CHAPTER NINE

REVOLUTION FOR ECLECTICS

There is symmetry to the protest that surrounds the world today. It is protest gathered around a resurgent humanism. It is the individual railing against structures that seek to deny his being.

History has moved us from bands to tribes to cities to states to nations to blocs. The momentum of this movement could, conceivably, carry us to international forms and controls that could, at last, effectively cage our inner beasts. But now a tremor has begun to pass backward through the pattern. Nations risk their lives to disengage from blocs. States, cities, and economic units within some larger whole recoil from the insensitive bureaucracy of centralism. Community and ethnic groups within cities seek to reestablish identity and regain control of their lives. Within each of man's structures—his associations, religions, universities—the individual cries out for recognition. Even as we move politically toward those social forms needed to resolve the problems we share, our instinct for self-preservation alarms us to the devouring threat of bigness.

Wherever man challenges authority, he is attempting to gain identity. And wherever this challenge occurs—be it within a state, or a church, an institution, or even a value structure—it produces clamor.

No major social change has ever occurred without
clamor. We clamored for freedom as a nation, and won it.
We clamored for an end to slavery, and won that. We
clamored for decent working conditions and a share of the
economic action, and we won that. All three were clamorous,
upsetting epochs where our response fit the need.

What is the clamor for now? For peace. For true equality. For participation. For a deeper view of man.

Is it possible that we have reached a breakthrough in
our concepts? That enough people truly care about the plight
of the disaffected to join in an irresistible clamor for change?
That young people who challenge a two-dimensional role for
men are in such a position that they can be the first generation to carry their ideals, unblemished, through the trials and
temptations of adult apprenticeship—and by implanting
these ideals in *their* time of leadership—produce a setting for
men of depth?

Clamor makes noise, scares people, provokes reaction.
But is this not what the clamor's about? And if we believe
in peace, equality, and a multidimensional life, then clamor
is cause for cheers, not wails—particularly when evidence
mounts that responsible clamor effectively catalyzes action.

What is "responsible clamor?" It is protest that by its
conviction, its truths, its manifest energy, and its dignity
eventually wins minds to its cause. It is not bombings and
killings that, however morally inspired, threaten the very
objectives in whose cause they are invoked.

History will show that in the summer of 1970, irrespon-
sible protest—the random killing of police officers, the bomb-
ing of a mathematics research center at the University of
Wisconsin—called down an indiscriminate repression on the
radical American left, guilty and innocent alike. History will

also show that prior to that time, responsible clamor had permanently altered America.

It has introduced skepticism into the bland, accepting patterns of American life.

It has made pacifism respectable.

It has challenged the idea of war.

It has challenged the nature of work and education in America, believing that there is more to life than to grow up, make money, and die.

It has articulated black rage in such a way that it can never be mistaken or forgotten again.

In less than a generation, it has found its way back from the beat life on the road to the very heart of the American experience. In 1964, the best that Democratic reformists could manage was a fight over who would occupy the seats of the Mississippi delegation. In 1968 they compelled an abdication.

Responsible black clamor is necessary, in that it achieves catharsis for the black man and redemption for the white man before the rage becomes so overwhelming that it ceases to be articulate and must be overcome to achieve survival.

Responsible student clamor is necessary, in that it startles educators out of deep academic ruts and compels us all to re-evaluate the purpose for which man exists.

Our extremists are the inventors of action to see what happens. Perhaps, however much we may know of the hazard of reaction born of purely anarchic clamor, a measure of such was required to dislodge majority thought.

Now that the energy has been spent and the passions aroused, it seems all but inconceivable that we have had to riot against one another to establish the idea that man ought to be the sum of his parts, rather than a mechanism defined by a function. Only a fool would dispute the idea that a whole man—embodying culture, service, aesthetics, leisure, love—is better than the man whose brain dedicates its conscious and unconscious energies to the improvement of a product. Yet it has taken riots.

Where the extremists have erred is in leaving the feeling that there's nothing to believe in, when there is, beginning with the growth of disbelief itself.

Disbelief is essential, until it becomes so destructive and powerful as to cause disbelievers to disbelieve in themselves, in other human beings, and in the capacity for change.

Revolt for the sake of revolution—let's do it and see what happens—so antagonizes and disgusts the rest of society that it negates the possibility of social compact.

But revolution for eclectics is a viable means of reform.

The dictionary tells us that eclectics are "liberal," "unfettered," "broad in matters of taste and belief." They would recoil from extremes and absolutes, but not from the discovery of need. Because they are accustomed to collecting truths from different systems, eclectics not only have a disposition for synthesis, they are the infantry of change.

This is how they reason:

Our response to problems moves along a single track when, in fact, several are available. We think in terms of absolutes when we might ponder shades and mixes. Solutions to problems are not necessarily either/or propositions; they are often a bit of this and that.

People constantly look for an absolute truth that eliminates all other truths, when truth, in fact, may come from many sources. They are constantly suggesting that one way is better than another way, when both ways may serve a cause. Now that private enterprise had discovered our social dilemmas, the Republicans among us cheer it as a means of deliverance from welfare. It won't deliver us, but it will help us and it ought to be employed—along with government programs. (We should not delude ourselves that we are saving any money if we give tax credits and subsidies to private enterprise to do the job. Both are forms of government spending.) We debate endlessly over central power versus local power, when the power of each is required. The proper debate is whether central power sufficiently expresses our vision and local power so engages our muscle that all of us feel involved.

What we are witnessing historically is the cresting of the collective urge. Yet anarchy, its antithesis, has never been less appropriate. We are beginning to see the effects of an unchecked population program—starvation that could spread through the underdeveloped parts of the world and lead to human chaos. Once already, we have gone to the brink of nuclear war. We have been given a deadline—within the lifetime of most of us—for when our wastes will finally kill all living things. Never has there been a greater need for ample thoughts and acts. Somehow, this need must be combined with individual self-realization into some kind of encompassing truth.

A round truth includes an element so skeptical of authority or government or "progress" that it compels those at the head to think many times before they move.

A round truth includes certain unassailable standards—that no man should starve or live a life of indignity or impose his will on others, and that any system that does any of these things ought to be changed.

A round truth includes the recognition that there is a place for responsible clamor which obviously must grow ever louder until it attracts attention to the injustice it protests.

A round truth includes forces in apparent contradiction that are valid and essential at once—increased centralization where it is clear that no private or smaller power can cope or is willing to; increased decentralization where the individual and the purpose become lost in the function.

Some of us draw up charts comparing events today with those of one hundred to one hundred and fifty years ago. Russia in 1848 was crushing revolutions in Central Europe. Frenchmen overthrew their king and established a republic, only to have their first president proclaim himself an emperor. Pius IX entered office a supposed progressive, then took refuge on the right to ward off change. It all sounds so similar—and yet it is all so different because the ingredients are different.

If you believe in man, then you must believe in the historical process. But I do not mean the fatalistic cyclical processes proposed by the historical determinists. I mean the historical progress of man himself, a process that is dynamic and changing, able to absorb, encompass, grasp, and utilize the incredible discoveries—technological, aesthetic, psychological, even political—that are showering down upon us like gifts.

There are all sorts of devices in society that compel us to reverse our ideas about which way man is going. It is no longer necessary to imprison ourselves further in deterministic historical prophecies about man. Scientific breakthroughs have changed all of man's options and prospects. To say that because Greek and Roman empires failed, Western culture is cyclical as well, is to deny the evidence that this culture is opening up geometric rather than arithmetic distances between itself and the fate of empires.

"The metaphor of growth contains immense nostalgia for living things and their fate as well as a sense of purposeful development," writes J. H. Plumb, professor of modern history at Cambridge. "It pervades literature, painting, music as well as political and social theory. Nor is this in any way surprising: we have been living for the last 6.5 thousand years in a dominantly agrarian society, varying in complexity and overlaid at different depths with craft, commerce and industry.

"It is, therefore, to be expected that there should be resonances, echoes, common chords and even similar symphonic themes in the ideas that men have developed by men about their destiny. Nor is it surprising that the most fundamental should be the metaphor of growth and decay which, to stress a banality, is his own experience of life.

"The end of this metaphor may be [near]; for, as we begin to move into a full scientific and technological world, a process that historically speaking has only just begun, it is possible than man's concepts of his destiny will change fundamentally and that old metaphors will die, just as there are signs that the power of socially manufactured pasts with their sanctions for morality and institutions are also dying."

It is as though the game has suddenly been taken away from the coaches and given back to the players.

What is the players' will now?

What *is* the relationship of the Backlash American to the Silent American to the Middle American to the Radical American? What *is* the nature of their thought, and how, if at all, does it differ from a generation or two ago?

There comes a point in protest when several things begin to happen. First, a wave of reaction sets in among an element that is insensitive to social problems. Second, the protest itself is contained by force. Third, even those who champion the objectives of change may become disaffected.

But the final thing that happens is the kind of thing Lew Douglass was talking about. The wrong about which the militants were protesting remains to haunt those who put down the protest; the only way this ghost can be exorcised is to remove the condition it has come to haunt.

Can men exorcise their ghosts? Or must existence always be haunted? What can men do against the structures that arise inexorably from their ranks? Are they masters of their own fate, or are they captives of their most base instincts, expressed by the most powerful among them? This is *the* eternal struggle. It is the status of this struggle that must be measured to see where men are today.

The great, historic accounting is that men believe today, as they have never believed before, that they can affect their environment. They believe it because they are.

"We are neither psychologically predestined to fulfill the imprinting of childhood trauma nor are we creatures who march blindly to the roll of society's drum," says Theodore Lidz, chairman of the department of psychiatry at Yale University's School of Medicine. "From the day of our birth to the night of our death, we are shaped by, and we in turn shape, the world in which we live."

Each of us carries in him all the positive and negative forces that characterize a society. We can argue forever about what man is. We can ultimately agree that left to his own devices, man might act selfishly, no matter how he might hurt others. But the point is not what man is, but what he has *become*. He is not what he was fifty years ago, and he will not be fifty years from now what he is today. He constantly improves his understanding of himself, and how he must harmonize what he is to what he must be in order to live in the world.

The fight for the world is the large stage of the fight between the good and evil in man. Whether man, if left to himself, would act in selfish ways, is practically irrelevant.

The moment he socializes, he begins to organize life for the common survival.

The ideal society is composed of an educated electorate that knows how to make government conform to its will. That society begins to form when men discover themselves.

This new generation's claims to the contrary, self-discovery is not its invention. Man's realization that whatever made him, made him responsible for himself has been emerging throughout time.

"Who is God?" a young West Indian friend once demanded of the novelist Frank Harris.

"He made the world," Harris answered.

"Who made God?" the West Indian asked then.

Harris turned away, stricken. His faith fell apart. Months later it returned, in a vastly altered form. Harris discovered beauty, in the world, in himself.

"Faith had left me, and with faith, hope in heaven or indeed in any future existence. Saddened and fearful, I was as one in prison with an undetermined sentence; but now in a moment, the prison had become a paradise, the walls of the actual had fallen away into frames of entrancing pictures. Dimly I became conscious that if this life were sordid and mean, petty and unpleasant, the fault was in myself and in my blindness. I began then for the first time to understand that I myself was a magician and could create my own fairyland, ay, and my own heaven, transforming this world into the throneroom of a god!" Harris developed a new faith that guided all his mature life. "Very soon the first command of it came to my lips almost every hour: 'Blame your own blindness! Always blame yourself.' "

Man blames himself today as he never has before.

Man today is seeking, not escaping from freedom. He is refusing to accept the reality he inherits. He is trying to change reality. It is interesting, and transiently important, that he is being resisted. It is enduringly important that much of what he is attempting today he was not attempting twenty years ago.

We must measure the evolution of the whole man, rather than just the political man. The politician may kill man before man can gain control of his world. But man ought to be given credit for trying. Twenty years ago we were crying that science had outraced ethics, that man was no longer capable of controlling the world, but only of destroying himself. The disorder of recent years is exactly this: man's attempt to find an ethic to match his times.

I'm not suggesting that the world is redeemed. I'm simply saying that it isn't necessarily doomed.

I'm not suggesting the world is perfect. I am suggesting that our problems have at last been identified, measured, and recognized; that such a population exists both in terms of numbers and influence that will not accept conditions as they are; that this population guarantees the continuity of change and that political forms must eventually bend to its will.

What is needed is a constructive element that will follow the path challenge opens up. When these two elements are working together, we have progress.

Progress requires more than challenge. It requires a force to solidify change. That force is building now.

Our society has reversed a critical element of the historical process. The elite in encrusted societies have traditionally neutralized rebels with an embrace. Our elite is different because what constitutes it is different; it is an elite not of property but of brains. *Our* historical process witnesses the elite's slow, steady, irrevocable embrace of the mass by the force of education.

"What the advanced nations have done," says Kenneth

Keniston, associate professor of psychology at Yale, "is to create their own critics on a mass basis—that is, to create an ever-larger group of young people who take the highest values of their societies as their own, who internalize these values and identify them with their own best selves, and who are willing to struggle to implement them."

Today, the force of education even just measured in numbers must eventually affect the historical order. As Frederick Rudolph, Mark Hopkins Professor of American History at Williams College, states:

> The recent upheavals on American campuses are not simply temporary and unpleasant incidents perpetrated by vicious enemies of the social order. The riots may indeed record a social, economic and political revolution, but fundamentally they are manifestations of the emergence of the university as the central institution in modern democratic liberal society. The military-industrial state cannot exist without it; an informed and imaginative electorate, sensitive to the conditions necessary to sustain human life and spirit, is impossible without it; attacks on the indifference and criminality that have bred our ghettos and rural slums, polluted our air and water and poisoned social life will get nowhere without it. The prospects of American civilization—and all that means for our friends and critics elsewhere—are now entrusted to the universities. They are the guardians of humane action.

So, the university may quite soon become what Harold Taylor calls "a permanent source of social change."

Ten years from now, our voting lists will be augmented by between 15 and 20 million Americans who will have shared the common experience of university life in the 70s; in effect, they will have supplanted as voters some 12 to 15 million Americans who shared no such experience. These variously educated new voters will not all think alike, and they will not vote as a bloc, but everything that is happening on the campus instructs us that they will share certain broad values with compelling moral force.

One day, there will be an "educated" majority in the United States; an educated political base will exist.

What will be its beliefs?

What ethic will it find to match its problems? What ideas will this mass of people presumably blessed more richly than any other anywhere at any time chisel into stone?

At the risk of the ultimate chutzpah, I'd like to propose a few:

• All rational men own a morsel of truth.

• Ask, first, not what is wrong with what another man is saying, but what is right. There is time enough to ask what's wrong.

• Recognize that when you win, someone loses who lives for the day he will win.

The prerequisite of any enduring relationship is equality. As Jean Monnet, the architect of European unity, once told me, "You can unite what is equal. You can't unite what isn't equal."

This is the point where new ethic and old problem fuse into an idea sufficiently original to match its task. It is an idea whose mounting requires a whole new attitude toward conquest. It is an idea that could only be held by men with an adequate sense of themselves.

Everything really does begin with how men felt about themselves until only very recently, and how they feel today. If no man can reach beyond his defenses until he believes in himself, neither can peoples or countries. People must succeed on their own terms; only that confirms them. The students clamoring for manhood on the campus, the devout clamoring for selfhood in their church, the peoples of underdeveloped countries wanting to make it themselves are none of them different from what our blacks want and need in America. Confirmation is the essential prerequisite to emotional and political peace.

Once we accept ourselves, we have no need to impose ourselves. The generation growing up today acts the way it does because it feels no guilt, accepts itself, and has no need to dominate.

The old idea that "we" must win and "they" must lose builds disaster into the political process. Both must win—not draw, win.

Failure breeds tension and suspicion. Success, broadly shared, could exorcise the ghost of political competition from international affairs. Peaceful competition works excellence from peoples. Political competition kills them.

There is only one valid battle—each man's to be himself. There are several routes to that vital center where man can pursue his quest confirmed by the gathering evidence of victory of the good over the evil within him. The evidence is the world he makes. It is no accident that he winds up at its core. The center is where opposites converge.

If that center were static it would be no place for man. But convergence becomes dynamic when that center moves. It is man himself who changes, and changing, moves the world.

POSTSCRIPT

Linden, Jeff:

All generations build a bridge, between those before and after themselves. My parents' generation did it, mine is doing it, and yours will do it, too.

We bridge-builders need passionate people behind us, mocking, goading, insisting, "Build that bridge! Build it!" Otherwise it might not get built. But as a builder of structural bridges might suspect two jutting geological lips as foundations for his span, my generation has tended to suspect political extremes as platforms for its bridge. We have learned that what can't bear bridges can't bear truth.

Our generation has confronted every imaginable extreme and survived them all. Meanwhile, we have quietly built our bridge. It is a long and complex structure, surely the most complex ever made. But I suspect it will be nothing compared to yours. Yours will not merely be very different from any bridge that has ever been built, but the most daring human structure ever conceived. To tell you why I must tell you a story that I've never told before. It isn't the easiest story to tell because it resurrects some unpleasant times. But it's a story I must pass to you because it encapsules all that I've learned. I don't wish to sound overblown; it's simply that, to learn this lesson, I paid an unusual price. I'd like you to have it free.

When I was thirty-four, I had to confront the possibility that I might not live to be thirty-five. A few months later, I had to come to terms with the realization that I had suffered a needless operation and lost a vital organ I might someday need to survive.

One Sunday in January, 1963, one of those incredible Brazilian days that heat the body and soothe the mind, a day in which I have never, ever felt better in my life, I began to bleed from somewhere inside myself. It took three writhing sessions on the surgical table of a Brazilian doctor, without anesthesia of any kind, to determine the source of the bleeding. It was from my left kidney.

Cancer? Certainly not. Well, probably not. In all probability, not. But if you're going to the States . . .

Then, a freak coincidence. A call from New York. An assignment there. Up I went, X-rays in hand.

Shakes of the head. Shrugs of the shoulder. An accidental meeting at a party with a specialist, the husband of a friend. To Hartford for a new test that had never erred before. I flunked.

If that test and two others made at Mount Sinai Hospital in New York were to be believed, my left kidney carried a malignant tumor. If other tests were to be trusted, it did not.

How could I know? There were two alternatives. I could wait three months and repeat the tests. Or I could undergo exploratory surgery. If I waited? Well, if you do have cancer, the wait could kill you. And if we explore? You could lose the kidney. Three chances in ten. On the other hand, five persons in every thousand are born with one kidney and live full normal lives.

And so I agreed to the exploratory operation. And I lost a kidney.

Afterward as I lay in my hospital bed, I explored the new psychological growth.

Not for a moment had I been frightened of death. Death, I saw, was something utterly without properties, a condition that could be defined not by what is, but only by what is not. Death is not-life, not-living; by itself it is nothing. Thus, the pain of death is not related to the condition of death itself, but rather to the end of what is real: life. Because life for me is so extraordinary, death, as an act of deprivation of extraordinary life becomes a dreadful robbery. One can be bitter about losing what transcends value—life— one can be angry, upset, grim, sorrowful, even mournful. But one can certainly never be frightened.

Months later, the fright came: a fright that made me wonder whether I could hold on to my mind. Each step taken for all the right reasons, and leading closer to the wrong answer. Each incriminating test giving off signals exactly like those of a malignant tumor that did not in fact exist.

I began to replay the past, to refuse that assignment, not go to that party, make the illogical, unsafe choice. It didn't work, and the terror grew, because for the first time in my life I felt I was vulnerable to events I could not control.

It was a discovery more infinitely terrifying than the prospect of death. If I could be frightened not by the thought of death, but by the thought of a life I did not totally control, what, I had to ask myself, had I done to control life?

The answer was simple. I had created a world I controlled—a small, telescoped world that excluded uncertainty. I had created a prison. I had been dead in life.

I wish I could write now that my costly discovery set me free. La, but I wrote some pretty things at the time. I was through with envy. I would no longer set my life to the standards of others; my goals, henceforth, would be my own. And so forth. No. It's not true. The man who starts a game at thirty-five will never be the champion.

But he will play better that he would have had he never played at all. And so, if I haven't kicked envy, I am at least quicker to recognize its symptoms, and check my wayward course. If I am still partnered to society's standards, I am no longer a silent partner. I do what I can to affect those standards—even at risk to myself.

Because there is one thing that I did get for my kidney. I learned to accept uncertainty. From that time to this, I have known that only when I'm uncertain am I certain that I'm alive.

Most people flee from uncertainty. Uncertainty is now my friend. Each step forward pokes the horizon two steps back. But look at the ground I expose.

If this generation has inherited anything from mine, I think it is precisely here. It accepts as a given what I had to learn. Uncertainty is its friends.

Perhaps Vietnam was its kidney.

This generation does not fear change. It seeks change as a way of life.

We have permitted the most activist and least palatable elements of the new generation to identify its character. They have served a purpose, but their function is limited; they would envelop us in anarchic individualism, the most deadly conformity of all.

Do we judge a generation by its warts or by its beauty marks, as well? The generation I know—the generation that my generation made—this generation has been set free in a way none other ever has. And it is a beautiful sight to behold.

You are the first, the very first, not to seek the components of certainty as your major task in life. And so you have a greater chance than any of us ever had to really change the world. The ideal, we've said, is an educated electorate that knows how to make government conform to its will. When that electorate finds more value in uncertainty than in certainty, then it is in a position to make demands on society in ways that have never occurred before. It will be willing to risk, because the classical punishments of nonconformity—the lower salary, delayed advancement, the smaller house, and diminished status—will be more than compensated for by the sense of freedom and community, and of spiritual self-fulfillment. When that electorate, with its greater feeling for groups, expresses this feeling through governmental service, then, and only then, will government reflect its ideals.

We invented nothing, nor have you. You inherit the generational tradition at a time when change in all ways is possible at last, at a time when enlightenment in all forms has made that fact so well known to those who will profit most from change that they compel it irresistibly. They will have it, because you will help them.

Your cry is not revolution, but revolutionary change, not disorder but reorder, not a new kind of tyranny but a new kind of justice.

Be careful, my loves. There are men about with a seductive message that has existed since classical times: society is best served when those best equipped to serve it conduct its affairs. By whatever name that idea has passed, by whatever costume it has masqueraded, it has led, in the end, to tyranny. There are men today who say private power has become so vast that equal power is required to thwart it. The power they propose is "enlightened" dictatorship. Beware. Accept this much from your father: Society is best served when society serves itself.

A few days before the moment in which I write, our Brazilian friend Hermano Alves surfaced in Paris as a political exile. When I first knew Hermano, he was a wise and cynical journalist to whom other journalists turned for help. (He is the man who, that day in São Paulo, said the Alliance for Progress was dead but the journalists were afraid to write its obituary—thereby taunting them into obituaries.) Hermano is too good-humored to hate; he did not hate the United States. He simply found it wanting in understanding. A few years after I left Brazil, he was elected to the Brazilian Congress. He fought hard for the remnants of Brazilian democracy. One day Brazilian soldiers came to his house to arrest him. Somehow he escaped. He lived a clandestine, underground life in São Paulo and Rio, and one day, heavily disguised, walked into the Mexican Embassy. Several months later, the Papal Nuncio arranged for his safe conduct, and his family's, from Brazil. Then the Algerians invited him to come live there, and promised him a job. He arrived. Months passed without word. Finally, one day it came. The Algerians wanted him to work for them in counterespionage. At this point in his story Hermano laughed, "I did not pass all my life to wind up working for some third-rate CIA." He paused.

"You know, let me tell you. I have now seen it all. And do you know where is the best society in the world? Yours." He laughed again. "All that fighting for a better society. It's beautiful. Beautiful!"

Go home, beloveds, and fight for a better society.

Dad

"Brothers, to arms! For a great darkness chokes the earth;
I say that day will dawn—would I were still alive—when both
our gods—without, within—shall come to grips! And then, my
lads, joy to that man who'll still be here to throw his cap high
in the flaming air and give the signal!"

—*The Odyssey: A Modern Sequel* by Nikos Kazantzakis

Thank You

Gardner Cowles and William B. Arthur, for the voyages that helped make this book, and for permission to use materials from you.

Irwin Shaw; Vance Packard; Robert K. Massie; Harold Evans, editor of London's *Sunday Times;* John Flint, associate editor, *The Reader's Digest,* Paris office; Frederick C. Painton, Paris correspondent, *U.S. News & World Report;* Hywel Jones, economist, Cambridge University; Earl A. Loomis, Jr., M.D., psychiatrist, New York City; Lester Libo, professor of psychology, University of New Mexico Medical School; Richard and Lee Jessor, professors of psychology, University of Colorado; A. Robert Towbin, financier; and anonymous officers of the U.S. Foreign Service, for your encouragement and suggestions.

Evan Thomas, my editor at W. W. Norton & Company, for the interest that provoked this book, and for your subsequent patience, gentle persistence, and balance.

Sterling Lord, for help no client should expect of an agent.

Nancy K. Goell, for research; Pucci Meyer and Melinda Moon, for typing.

And my family, for enduring, since 1968, the unwitting discourtesies of a reporter in the process of asking himself whether he had been to the right places, seen the right things, and taken from them what he should.

LEONARD GROSS